PASTORAL CARE AND COUNSELING

PASTORAL CARE
AND
COUNSELING
AN INTRODUCTION

Care for Stories, Systems, and Selves

Philip Browning Helsel

Paulist Press
New York / Mahwah, NJ

Cover image by Jassy 77777 / Shutterstock.com
Cover and book design by Lynn Else

Library of Congress Cataloging-in-Publication Data
Names: Helsel, Philip Browning, author.
Title: Pastoral care and counseling : an introduction : care for stories, systems, and selves / Philip Browning Helsel.
Description: New York : Paulist Press, [2019] | Includes bibliographical references and index.
Identifiers: LCCN 2018018804 (print) | LCCN 2018039574 (ebook) | ISBN 9781587687617 (ebook) | ISBN 9780809153909 (paperback :alk. paper)
Subjects: LCSH: Pastoral care. | Pastoral counseling. | Caring—Religious aspects—Christianity.
Classification: LCC BV4011.3 (ebook) | LCC BV4011.3 .H454 2019 (print) | DDC 253—dc23
LC record available at https://lccn.loc.gov/2018018804

ISBN 978-0-8091-5390-9 (paperback)
ISBN 978-1-58768-761-7 (e-book)

Published by Paulist Press
997 Macarthur Boulevard
Mahwah, New Jersey 07430

www.paulistpress.com

Printed and bound in the
United States of America

To my parents, Marvin Helsel Jr. and Karen Helsel, who,
throughout their years of ministry, taught me to look
at the world through the eyes of faith

CONTENTS

ACKNOWLEDGMENTS

I am grateful for the many voices that have guided me on the way and for the wisdom of churches and parishes that have shaped me. I have attended many churches where profound pastoral care was already underway, almost despite the leadership. This book is in honor of what they already do.

I have also benefited from concrete, kind, and practical guidance from pastoral supervisors, such as Peggy Fullman, may she rest in peace, Cindy Bowman, and Peter Stimpson. These ministers taught me to accompany others with wisdom. I am grateful to Gary Charles and his ministry of social justice, as well as the domestic violence shelter where I volunteered with abused children in college, where I learned what it meant to leave violence. Everyday ministry supervision taught me about prayerful pastoral care amid life's extremities.

I am thankful for those pastoral theologians who, in recent years, have argued that the parish and congregation are worthwhile places to reflect on pastoral care, especially Cedric Johnson, Lee Ann Fuller, Karen Scheib, Larry Kent Graham, rest his soul, and Rodney Hunter, among others.

I thank God for my students. I have taught this material in various forms since 2012 when I pioneered my introductory course, "Care for Stories, Systems, and Self." My students at Boston College School of Theology and Ministry and at Austin Presbyterian Theological Seminary, where I currently teach, have helped me explore what God's sustaining presence means in times of intense suffering. Churches in Boston and Austin have been audiences for this material in Sunday school and church retreats. I am grateful for their open hearts and clear thinking in conversation with the ideas of this book.

PASTORAL CARE AND COUNSELING

The seminary faculty, administration, and staff at Austin Seminary gave a generous sabbatical to work on this material and shaped the ecclesial imagination that undergirds it. Our faculty assistant, Candace Mathis, helped me write for the church, and her tireless labor has been one of the most important forces leading to this book. "Faculty meeting" offered a forum for improvisation. Austin Seminary supported my work as a faculty member writing for lay theologians in the pews.

The group of New Directions in Pastoral Theology at Princeton Seminary, led by my dissertation advisor, Robert C. Dykstra, was an annual encouragement to keep writing and a forum for publication. This group also encouraged attention to many of the themes in this volume.

In an era in which so many people leave the church and never come back, this book might seem anachronistic. Nevertheless, I argue for the gifts of the church and its ongoing edification; may it thrive, be healed from its sins, and continue to transform the world through Christ's presence.

In closing, I express gratitude to God for answered and unanswered prayer, for everyday meetings with grace, and the meeting of basic needs. My wife, Carolyn, has been supportive and my children, Caleb and Evelyn, have kept me playing. The birds God created continue to bless with their light yoke.

INTRODUCTION

Ministers are often on the front lines of social suffering, engaging in pastoral care with people who are struggling with trauma, mental illness, addiction, and other difficulties. Ministers face such problems at a higher rate today than they have in the past.

Ministers engage with stories *because they believe that people are more than their problems.* In fact, through helping people unfold their distinctive stories and heal their broken systems, ministers can help them believe that they are remembered by God amid their suffering. It is the nature of this work that is taxing, and ministers need to practice care for their own stories so that they can engage effectively with the difficulties they encounter.

The ideas presented here are intended primarily for people who are becoming familiar with the field of pastoral care and counseling for the first time, but it can also reorient experienced practitioners of pastoral care by helping them care *for Stories, for Systems,* and *for Selves.* While the ideas are presented for the newcomer to the discipline, the linking of the three concepts — care for stories, systems, and self — is intended for all practitioners.

This book is divided into three parts: Care for Stories, Care for Systems, and Care for Selves. All aspects are inextricably connected within the call to ministry. Central to the book is the idea of listening for stories and witnessing to them as an act of faith. The call begins at baptism, its purpose is to engage in various forms of service to the church and world as a response to God's faithfulness in Jesus Christ.

At the outset, it is helpful to define *careseekers* and *caregivers* in the context of ministry. *Careseekers,* also called counselees or clients, are those who come to a minister for help with personal difficulties, many of which have a social component. Counselees and clients seek out specialized help for their problems. *Caregivers* are called and confirmed within a specific community to which they are held accountable. Some ministers are ordained and serve priestly or preaching functions, while others are responsible for the care and fiscal leadership of their communities. Throughout, I emphasize the similarities between lay and ordained clergy in the activities of pastoral care and counseling. I will not give sustained attention to questions of the definitions of ministry, as this has been done elsewhere.[1]

A central idea is that pastoral care and counseling takes time. Many of the sources of suffering described, from addiction to suicide, are not simplistic problems that can be dealt with in a formulaic fashion. Rather, ministerial responses to all difficulties require patient dwelling within the complexity of human experience. Pastoral care and counseling invites this seldom-lauded theological virtue of *patience*, which consists of wisdom and fortitude on the part of the caregiver.

We challenge the quick-fix culture and argue that accompaniment is better suited to pastoral life than a problem-solving orientation. Since the average person suffering from addiction will enter as many as ten to twenty-five rehabilitation programs before recovering, a model of accompaniment is necessary. Likewise, battered spouses typically take eleven and a half years to leave their partners, a fact that demands ministerial sensitivity and wisdom. While ministers may be drawn to quick-fix solutions, they also need to plan for healing, which takes time.

Because of time constraints and the confusing nature of pastoral boundaries, ministers can only do so much of the pastoral care in their religious community. For this reason, ministers need to educate and support the concerned lay caregivers that are already engaged in ministry in their religious community. One congregation I served had an energetic deacon who would clean the ovens of elderly homebound women in the church who did not have money to hire help (see chapter 2).

Drawing from the wellspring of religious practice, pastoral care and counseling may seem like a technical discipline but, in fact, it is closer to a concrete act of service such as this deacon provided. Service is at the heart of pastoral care and counseling, and for wise pastoral care to occur, it is important to develop ways of communicating about pastoral care in congregations and support the excellent pastoral care already present in religious communities.

Each pastoral care encounter is a moment in which theology is engaged anew and fresh knowledge is created. When elderly persons feel forgotten in a nursing home and a volunteer brings them the sacrament, the community begins to be healed by being re-membered, the body of Christ connecting with the unified body of the community in a moment of theological creation. By forgetting them, the community is dismembered temporarily; by incorporating them again, the community becomes itself more completely.

Everyday situations of alcoholism, suicide, and child abuse call for theological responses. Listening is such a response. Careful listening helps transform these scenes of human suffering and creates a new knowledge of God. Just by truthfully witnessing to the scenarios without succumbing to the natural human tendency to avoid pain, caregivers display a glimpse of God's faithfulness and mercy. In these circumstances, people ask questions about the presence of God in suffering and wonder why terrible things happen to good people. They also may struggle with their own sin and shortcomings. At times, people ask if they need to forgive an abusive family member to be forgiven by God. At other times, they notice the mystery and wonder of God through unexpected consolation in prayer.

Pastoral care and counseling are grateful responses to the gracious gift of God. God's grace comes first in every human encounter, and pastoral caregivers seek to make sense of suffering and so discern the presence of God's Spirit. Ministers who remain engaged in situations of suffering help people make meaning even if they never attempt to answer the profound theological questions that are asked. Simply allowing the space for questions to be asked is a profound form of ministry. Likewise, unless God is already present and acting in that person's life, ministry will be impossible.

Every act of ministry involves balancing the needs of suffering people, the communal requirements of leadership and administration, and the needs of a world crying out for justice. One of the important facets of ministry is balancing care for the religious community with care for social problems in one's town and region. Answering emails, balancing budgets, and allocating mission funds are all activities of pastoral care, broadly understood since fiscal propriety is part of wise and ethical ministry that helps religious communities continue practices of care.

Pastoral care and counseling is used to help communities searching for theological sense amid life's most intractable difficulties. This book offers skills and resources to move from a problem-oriented approach into an approach that dwells with discernment for God's presence in life's difficulties. Pastoral care and counseling is always public ministry, and, as the quality of their activities quickly becomes well known in the community, further requests for pastoral care are made.

THREE INTERLOCKING THEMES

Care for stories means that we attend to the distinctive meanings that a person has made from their own life. When ministers do story care, they help people feel remembered by God. Even listening with attention to the shape of one person's story, especially if it has been silenced, is an act of justice. Care for stories has a priority here, and it is a complex and demanding work of justice and mercy.

Care for systems means that we treat the systems that we wish to change as capable of changing, whether a government bureaucracy, a health care system, or a prison system. It also means that the major problems people face, such as addiction, relate to the family and social systems in which people live, and that treatment must be a systemic reality. By working for system-wide transformation, ministers become advocates. Each of the stories in this book, however personal, has a social context that impacts its expression. When ministers practice systemic care, they help people live up to their full potential and honor one another. By emphasizing the systemic nature of all care, social and personal problems are frequently linked. For example, problem debt has been linked to suicide risk, and unemployment to missed days of work from depression. In every instance, personal problems are social and need to be addressed in a multidimensional way.

Care for selves means that each time a minister hears another person's story or attempts to change a system, the minister pays attention to embodied experience. They offer God's grace to themselves even as they become sad or angry from witnessing someone else's struggle. To engage in the care for stories with perseverance, ministers need to believe that their own stories are held by a compassionate God. Experiencing God's rest or Sabbath as a gift of time, ministers can slow down and develop a savoring pace that reflects God's mercies.

The approach of care for stories, systems, and selves builds upon each facet to make a flexible approach to pastoral care and counseling that can be used with wisdom. The order is logical. Story care is a priority since it is essential to all pastoral care. But beyond a pragmatic approach, the care for stories, systems, and self is inherently theological, becoming faithful as it balances all three important foci.

THE GOALS OF PASTORAL CARE AND COUNSELING

There are three important goals of pastoral care and counseling that are addressed by the care for stories, for systems, and for selves. The goals are for people to feel remembered by God in their circumstances, that they can challenge unjust suffering that has happened to them, and that they can have the freedom to participate more fully in the world around them. What makes pastoral care pastoral is that every act of care involves the process of crying out to God and seeking God's sustenance and presence.

The first goal of pastoral care is that persons need to have their stories heard so that they can ultimately conclude that God has been with them in their stories. This is why pastoral care is different from other forms of counseling: it is concerned with questions of God's faithfulness and not simply human meaning-making.

The second goal of pastoral care and counseling is to change the systems of a society so that more people can participate fully in decisions that matter to them. A communal element means individual counseling is not the only vision of pastoral care but should include activities such as working with social services as aspects of care. The first two goals belong together, and for this reason, the caregiver must always pay attention to the individual and the communal aspects of human experience.

The third goal of pastoral care is for the minister to experience God's faithfulness. This experience is the theological basis for self-care in ministry that requires attention to the minister's own story in her communal context. On the front lines of societal trauma, ministers risk burnout if they do not have adequate resources. On the front lines they need time to play, restore themselves, and experience God's direct and sustaining care.

The ethical orientation of pastoral care and counseling is toward the most *silenced stories* in communities of care because that is where God is distinctively at work. Many of the chapters include stories that may be taboo or passed over quickly in religious communities. By giving such narratives detailed attention, we make the argument that God is often at work in distinctive ways amid silenced human suffering.

Likewise, in congregational life, people without power are also silenced. When situations of conflict arise, and communities become tense, it can be important to ask whose stories are being neglected. Additionally, when we attend to these silenced stories, it means that God is unequivocally present in them, precisely because they are sites of marginalization.

DIGNITY AND VOCATION

Pastoral care and counseling takes place in relationship to God who created humans with dignity—inalienable worth regardless of their capacities, and *vocation*—a purpose that contributes to God's mission in the world. The relationships that ministers have with their parishioners and communities also reflect these twin poles of dignity and vocation.

At times, a minister's role is to cry out and grieve in public because of the pain that a religious community is facing. Since the word *care* is rooted in the Sanskrit meaning of "cry out" or "lament," it often occurs in moments of individual or community crisis when ministers lament to God on behalf of the people. As a crisis chaplain, I have helped a family cry out to God as an act of prophetic witness.

Care also occurs in moments of crisis in the minister's own story when individual hurt makes it difficult to continue giving care. Pastoral care and counseling is not simply about hearing individual stories so that people can feel accepted. It is about changing the conditions that marginalize them so that they can participate more fully in what matters most in their lives.

IMBALANCES IN STORY CARE

Not only is care for stories, systems, and selves theologically grounded; these foci also help stabilize pastoral care by fostering the appropriate balance of emphases. An emphasis on any one of the three facets of pastoral care, to the exclusion of the others, becomes lopsided, problematic, and eventually detrimental to the enterprise of pastoral care and counseling.

First, *an imbalance toward story care*. Perhaps the most common critique of pastoral care and counseling is that it is too individualistic.[2] For example, if a minister only cares for individual stories, that minister might give the impression that by just telling a life story in a different fashion, a careseeker can change their circumstances.[3] Frustratingly, expecting someone to pull themselves up by their bootstraps is not good story care. One-sided story care might not deal adequately with social factors such as poverty, marginalization, and prejudice that persist despite attention to the individual's story. Storytelling must be combined with the sense of empowerment to be authentic and effective. Nuanced story care means attending fully to what happened, to the contours of empowerment and blame that often arise in the sharing of stories, as well as to the opportunity for sensing future possibilities for one's actions.

Second, *an imbalance toward system care*. Some people are strongly oriented toward macro solutions that bring about change in the systems in which people live. If too much emphasis is laid on social change, a careseeker might feel that her distinctive story does not matter in the "big picture." Fatigued ministers may despair of ever changing society when they see the same social problems recurring. One minister who worked in a social service setting for several years attempted to bring about housing change in her community. Increasingly alienated from the church, she felt separated from her own resources of faith and identity as a minister and found that working as a parish associate helped restore her hope by caring for the faith of a community. In an exclusive focus on systems, individual voices are often drowned out and the emphasis is placed on the broad arcs of historical change. Nevertheless, without attention to the systems in which people live, pastoral care can seem ahistorical and out of touch. Caring for systems is an essential part of the healing of communities.

Third, *an imbalance toward self-care*. Talk of boundaries and professional ethics sometimes gives the impression that the self of the minister is fragile and must be guarded from suffering to prevent harm. Ministers also have privilege that comes from their ordination and community. If ministerial identity is only fragile, it might lead to a fearful orientation toward life and calling, seeing others as threats to be managed and a potential drain of energy. The paradox here is that even in trying to protect his integrity, the minister might distance himself from his own story and the system in which he belongs because of fear. One minister who had experienced childhood trauma became afraid when conflict erupted in his community. In trauma counseling, he began to be able to care for himself and thereby face the inevitable process of congregational conflict. Additionally, the care for self is an important part of every act of pastoral care because the good news of the gospel is just as important for the minister to hear for herself. Because of the central message that all are created in the image of God, each minister is "the apple of [God's] eye" regardless of what she can achieve or accomplish (Ps 17:8).

THE STRUCTURE OF THE BOOK

Each of the three sections—*care for stories, care for systems, and care for selves*—contains chapters, each telling a story about a care scenario that addresses a specific theme. Because such experiences have deep interpersonal textures, they lend themselves to a story format, and a series of chapters, with each unfolding into its own narrative. These narratives are drawn from what I have seen and experienced in various ministry contexts. Stories from the ministries of others, used by permission, will be referenced in citations. The concluding chapter draws together themes from the stories across the book to describe the dispositions and values of pastoral care and counseling.

The first three chapters of the book concern the care for stories. In the first chapter, we see how pastoral counseling is an activity that helps people feel remembered by God. Using Kevin's encounter with Pastor Janelle, I describe how Kevin had been facing chronic discouragement because of his factory's closure and difficult family dynamics as well as how Pastor Janelle showed pastoral imagination as she intervened by caring for attachment, time, context, and meaning-making in relationship to his story. Because she had the family backstory, she was able to help Kevin in a way that no secular counselor could have done, but the chapter also explains how to build a backstory if one does not have one. She balanced her own needs for self-care by being in spiritual direction, even as she hosted the pastoral conversations with Kevin, over a period of a few sessions.

In the second chapter, we unfold a pastoral care conversation in which Deacon Janine visited a parishioner, Margaret, and discussed her challenges with aging. The deacon not only listened to Margaret's story, she also stooped and cleaned her stove in an act of service. Here, we define *ministry* and distinguish pastoral care from pastoral counseling. This chapter is the central theoretical chapter pertaining to the care for stories, and it argues that everyday matters are the subject of pastoral care and counseling. Here too, pastoral care and counseling is set in a variety of contexts, the unconscious childhood motives behind ministry are explored, and a rationale is given why pastoral care is more like lament than encouragement. The chapter shows how sacred service takes place in the everyday care for ordinary matters.

By showing how Christ is present in our suffering, we can appreciate how the proper attitude of pastoral care is one of allowing lament to be voiced rather than being encouraging and changing the subject. Lament is one of the primary ways that the tenderness of God is expressed in human experience. We learn how a call to ministry can be built on unmet childhood needs, but that our personal needs must be explored and integrated to create a wiser ministry.

In chapter 3, we explore how attachment to God is impacted by the irruption of suicide. We learn from Ralph and June, parental survivors of an adolescent suicide, and how their survivors' image of God was shattered by the event. Father Bill helped Ralph and June lament to God and helped the religious community care for them rather than turn away from their suffering. Here, we see how suicide is a challenge to attachment, time, context, and meaning-making, and how ministers can help by enabling families to remember out loud other parts of their loved one's story aside from the suicide. The minister also helped the congregation to grieve and express their doubts, educating them in more compassionate pastoral responses.

The next section is about caring for the systems in which people live. The fourth chapter of the book explores how a church volunteer, Estela, meets Clara in their church food pantry. An undocumented day laborer, Clara has been fired from her job because of a workplace injury and cannot get compensation. The chapter explains how Estela works to find health care resources in her community, but also uses Clara's stories to open the empathic imagination of the entire church to the plight of undocumented immigrants. The story explains how Estela balances advocacy with compassionate listening. By challenging the communal narrative, she works to help the church imagine the undocumented as being created in God's own image.

The fifth chapter returns to Pastor Janelle from the first chapter and explains how she cares for Pam, Kevin's mother, a decade earlier.

The backstory of her advocacy for Pam indicates how the process of leaving an abusive relationship is, in fact, a faith story involving elements of one's spirituality and one that impacts the entire family. Those in abusive relationships are often trapped in multiple systems. Along with explaining how to accompany people who are leaving abusive relationships and how to educate religious communities about abuse, the story indicates how Pam's image of God is transformed through her encounter with Pastor Janelle. In what follows, the care for Pam's story is explored—including how her faith is related to her experience of abuse and how the broader problem of battering is placed in its social context—and advice is given for pastoral practice. In conclusion, the complicated issue of forgiveness is addressed. This story belongs in the systems section because the obstacles that battered spouses face are often enshrined in the court systems and other institutions. Those who face marginalization because of race, poverty, or immigration status have even more difficulty leaving an abusive relationship. Since women, who bear the dignity and vocation of the human person in equal measure to men, are disproportionately victimized simply because of their gender, helping them plan for safety is crucial to their spiritual lives.[4]

The sixth chapter of the book describes Samantha and her single father, James, as they struggle with Samantha's opioid addiction. Here, we address adolescent drug abuse as a systems issue, arguing that addiction is a spiritual habit as well as a response to family and social systems. Through the story of young addict Samantha, the chapter explains how addiction recovery requires both the development of life skills and the practice of a spirituality that can *replace* rather than *repress* the addictive urges.

The third section's chapters describe the care for self, the undergirding of all acts of ministry. The seventh chapter presents the story of Denise, a busy mother of young children who volunteers in the eucharistic ministry at the church. Her elderly father has been diagnosed with dementia and needs to be placed in a nursing home. Denise is fatigued by her many responsibilities. She takes time for a silent retreat and begins spiritual direction, activities that confirm for her that she is worth more than the role that she plays. She finds the gift of God's time that is the Sabbath. This chapter explains how self-care is a theological act, explores the reasons why people feel increasingly busy, examines middle generations caring for both children and parents, and offers spiritual practices that inform self-care. At the heart of this chapter is the love of God that reaches out to Denise, wanting to surround her with peace. The themes of this chapter can deepen and enrich self-care for a variety of pastoral caregivers whose circumstances may differ from those of Denise.

In the eighth chapter, we explore how to keep proper emotional and sexual boundaries in ministry. It tells the story of Father George and how he misuses his pastoral power by making sexual comments and sending an explicit text message to a recent divorcée who had become vulnerable with him in counseling. Emphasized is the need for full disclosure and a path to healing for the victim, the religious community, and the perpetrator, as is the need for confidentiality and its limits in pastoral counseling. Part of caring for the self means protecting the sacred boundaries of story care so that it can continue for a long time. In analyzing common ministerial boundary violations, this chapter provides a framework for the care for self that includes honoring the ethical sanctity of the stories of the careseeker while also caring for one's own stories. Those who have been the victims of clergy boundary violations may wish to read this chapter carefully, with special attention to the need for care of self.

Through the ninth and concluding chapter, we learn how the care being provided through ministers helps them integrate aspects of their own experiences and why such story care is holy. It reflects the image of God, indicating how people deserve dignity and respect, and it also underscores human vocation, showing how people are made with a purpose. While there are many stories throughout the book where people are mistreated, reducing them as a means to an end, we are reminded that pastoral care is a sacred practice that reclaims the human person as an end in itself. We find that it is marginalized people, adolescents, addicts, women, and undocumented persons who often have power used against them in oppressive ways. Many of the stories include different forms of grieving that are healed through an encounter with God's spirit, but the practices of ministry described here should be practiced in conjunction with other professionals such as ministers and counselors. The chapter is an effort to review some of the spiritual practices that have been addressed throughout and shows how they are ideally suited to the specific sociosystemic problems that are discussed.

This book arises from years of ministry in chaplaincy, congregational, and counseling settings, and so it is concerned with the difficult and rewarding work of pastoral care and counseling, which is always greater than any book can capture.

In the everyday life of a minister who seeks to help people engage the sacramental and worship life of their traditions, pastoral care is used in guidance and spiritual advice. This activity is an act of pastoral imagination, using the eyes of faith and the contours of experience to understand human suffering. In the process, ministers get a taste for what really matters, unfolding stories to discover the sacred in everyday life.

By contrast, pastoral counseling is an opportunity to look more deeply into the stories people tell with the hope of helping them with their difficulties. Pastoral counseling tends to be shorter term and focused on emotional difficulties or turning points in one's relationship to God in conversation; definitions are explained further in chapter 2.

Spiritual direction takes place in relationship to a director outside of one's circle of church or friendship who is specifically focused on helping one to increase spiritual practice in one's life, and so can be distinguished from pastoral care and counseling.

Revitalizing pastoral care and counseling allows us to bring all three factors into balance for the sake of wise, just, and compassionate ministry. It is my hope that, through this book, ministers will find new relevance in the field of pastoral care, those interested in social service work will understand its intersection with pastoral care, and all will find the hope that comes from remembering that God loves them unconditionally and equips them well for their vocation. Along the way, we will meet many practical examples that illuminate how to use the model of the care for stories, systems, and self successfully in practice in our calling by God.

I

CARE
FOR
STORIES

1

PASTORAL CARE CONVERSATIONS

Kevin seeks out his pastor, Janelle, because he is feeling discouraged. He has lost his job because of a factory closure and is back living with his parents in his childhood home. Although he attends community college part time, he is "having trouble getting things going." With big goals that do not seem to be materializing, he does not feel that he is measuring up. He says, "God is against me. Maybe I'm cursed." His slumped shoulders and downcast eyes tell her that he senses he does not have the right to take up space in this world. In telling his story, his whole body expresses the history of what has happened, only part of which he can put into words.

Why is Kevin seeking me for care right now? Pastor Janelle wonders to herself.[1] *What is the specific problem that brings him to see me? Even though he seems discouraged, why is he seeking a minister rather than a counselor and what does he want me to do for him?* Kevin's problems seem poorly defined. Nevertheless, she senses strong feelings when she talks with him. When she meets with Kevin, she believes that he is going through more than run-of-the-mill discouragement.

But Pastor Janelle also knows that Kevin's story is more complicated than he initially presents. Because Janelle has the broader context of his family dynamics in mind, she can listen to his narrative with more nuance and wisdom than a stranger in a clinical setting. She had the opportunity to counsel his mother nearly a decade ago amid marital complications, giving her resources for a domestic violence shelter when her husband had been abusing her. His mother never left the relationship, but she turned to Pastor Janelle for support periodically.

3

CARE FOR STORIES

Because Pastor Janelle understands something of his family history, she can see how deep his feelings run. Her "pastoral imagination" for Kevin's story is drawn from many years of engagement with his family, the church community, and the wider culture. Pastoral imagination is the hard-won insight that comes from years of engaging the multiple demands of ministry in conversation with Scripture and the worship life in a congregation. The seasoned wisdom that comes from this activity is a form of discernment that can be enriched through training.[2]

Kevin was working at a factory, but the job closed in his town. Now he is back home and beginning community college, but is discouraged because the job prospects are so poor. He does not seem enthusiastic about his studies and considers leaving town because the region is economically depressed. *I wonder if Kevin has returned home explicitly to protect his mother from his father,* Pastor Janelle wonders.

There is more than meets the eye in Kevin's story. Pastor Janelle is uniquely positioned to discern this deeper perspective. Kevin reaches out to Pastor Janelle because he has a story to tell. His story might seem confusing because it is not obvious what he wants from her. It might lack clear heroes or a compelling plot, but when she sits down to listen to him, she cares for his story, giving him the distinctive sense that he is known and understood. The care for a person's story requires some knowledge of individual psychology but also awareness of the social realities in which people are embedded.

Janelle has a narrow window of time after Kevin seeks her out to listen to him effectively. Because of such engaged listening, she might be able to speak to his chronic discontent in a way that brings about change. It is impossible for her to know exactly where God is at this point in his journey. As his minister, she helps him explore the important stories that have shaped him so that he can discern a direction for the future.

This means discovering how Kevin is a person with *dignity*: created in the image of God regardless of how he can perform. It also means discovering his vocation: how he is called to commitment to something greater than himself. His vocation means his God-given purpose, something that only becomes apparent through discernment.

Amid Kevin's discouragement, Pastor Janelle can witness to God's presence. This requires attention to the meaning of faith, knowledge of the broader backstory in Kevin's family, awareness of the social factors shaping him, and attunement with the future to which God beckons him. As a minister, Janelle is a witness to God's presence in his story. Witnessing is possible even though Kevin may not see these things clearly for himself.

To be effective, pastoral care conversations need to address attachment, time, context, and meaning-making. Attachment means listening so that someone feels like they matter. Time means creating sacred time for listening that helps parishioners understand their own movement through time. Context includes the setting of pastoral conversation, the region in which it takes place, and the social location of each participant. Meaning-making is arriving at some new understanding about one's life that takes shape in a story. Each of these important tasks is indispensable to pastoral care, and as they develop together in conversation, they create the conditions for maturation and change.

ATTACHMENT

Attachment is the basic sense of safety that is created when someone listens to a story attentively. It is about fostering the connection between a minister and the one they counsel. Pastors can mirror nonverbal body language as they listen. Dietrich Bonhoeffer states,

> The first service that one owes to others in the fellowship consists in listening to them. Just as love to God begins with listening to God's Word, so the beginning of love for the community is learning to listen to them. It is God's love for us that God not only gives us God's Word but also lends us God's ear. So it is God's work that we do for our brothers and sisters when we learn to listen to them. Christians... so often think that they must always contribute something when they are in the company of others, that this is the one service they have to render. They forget that listening can be a greater service than speaking.[3]

By listening to Kevin, Pastor Janelle helps him feel that he belongs somewhere. After their first conversation, he tells her, "Thank you for listening to me, it really helped." When people say something like this, they are saying that your relationship matters to them, not that you understand the content of a historical report. The dynamics of feeling supported arise from our early experiences of care at the hands of parents and guardians.

Being kept in mind by others is a powerful experience, and it can lead careseekers to feel that God keeps them in mind. In the first several years of life, a caregiver must attend to a child so that that child can feel *kept in mind* by others.[4] Mirroring a child's emotions and responding to his or her basic needs, the caregiver is laying down the foundation for the ability to perceive more accurately another person's thoughts, feelings, and intentions. If a person does not have this kind of mirroring in early life, an attentive minister like Pastor Janelle can respond in ways that help a person feel care.

As Kevin tries to leave home, he is impacted by family conflict in ways that reflect his childhood attachment. Pastor Janelle knows that his family fights and that his younger brother Evan ran away from home about five years ago. Although they look fine on the outside, there are times when this family is frightening to Kevin. Kevin's father, Sandy, used to come home after a night of drinking and throw things around the house, scaring the entire family. Pastor Janelle wonders if they live with a residue of fear. As noted earlier, a few years ago, she gave his mother, Pam, information about how to leave the relationship, urging her to seek safety at a local shelter.[5] Physical and emotional abuse are woven together in Kevin's life.

Fear is the constant companion in Kevin's family, and it seems to have impacted his self-image and even his faith. From an attachment perspective, Kevin might have had to cope with fear by avoiding it or fleeing it. He might believe that he is not able to protect those he loves from violence. Feeling helpless for much of his life may have created the condition where love is painful since one cannot protect one's family.

Pastor Janelle discerns that the adult Kevin feels worthless, and she wonders how this is related to his childhood and his current return to that childhood home. Just the week before, his father had made fun of him at the dining room table when they had guests visiting. His dad had called him a "loser" and a "failure." When messages of rejection pile up, it can make attachment difficult, which can thereby make moving forward in life harder.

A careseeker who finds such a healing relationship from a minister is psychologically indistinguishable from an individual who had such care early on from a primary caregiver. This means ruptures in an attachment relationship can be healed by later bonding. Those who do not find attachment from early caregivers can find a sense of belonging later in other supportive, mentoring relationships.[6]

In Kevin's case, for instance, Pastor Janelle's actions helped Kevin become more attached to his faith, even if he may not say so with his words. After pastoral conversations, Kevin visits the church several times a week, working on the garden in his spare time. By caring for the land and the physical location of the church, Kevin is able to give something back and connect to the place.[7] He shows an interest in helping with the sound system, something he is uniquely prepared for because of his prior factory work. Pastor Janelle understands that Kevin's interest in caring for church grounds might reflect one of the ways that he could express his faith in concrete terms, through actions of caring for something that he perceives as holy. The church can provide a haven for individuals in a world of rapid change, helping them to connect with other people that can show him respect despite his perceived failures. One way they do this is through attachment.

Attachment stems from early childhood caregivers who helped shape the mind by holding the body together, and it results in the feeling of being *kept in mind* by others. Such needs can be met in individual relationships as expressed in community. In Kevin's case, he found these needs being met through the Christian community of care and the physical place of the church property.

Everyone who seeks pastoral care tells a story, even if they barely speak. Each story also reflects patterns of attachment. A careseeker may seek a minister's help for reasons he may not even understand, often wanting to share some part of himself that he has not shared before.

Listening to a person's story helps establish closeness because it creates a connection between their experience and your response. Careseekers need to feel like there is a match between the truths they voice in pastoral care and a ministerial response. Kevin felt alone and discouraged about his career prospects. When Pastor Janelle hears him talk this way, she responds by matching his experience rather than changing the subject or moving him quickly toward an answer. This feeling of a match is a sign that attachment needs are being met through conversation.

Ministers engage in care and counseling to help distressed people feel remembered by God, God being the ultimate attachment figure.[8] Although Pastor Janelle does not explore Kevin's faith struggles right away, she speculates that there may be a spiritual reason why he seeks a minister for conversation rather than a therapist. When ministers listen with attention to the shape of a story, they implicitly help people feel that God keeps them in mind.

Children develop into maturity by being kept in mind by their caregivers. Likewise, in the journey of faith, feeling kept in mind amid our suffering can lead to hope. Scripture indicates that feeling remembered by God *as individuals* is equally important as being remembered in the community of faith. The Psalmist says, "Remember me, O LORD, when you show favor to your people" (Ps 106:4). Part of the reason why Kevin might feel the sustenance of faith through his conversation with Pastor Janelle is that, for him, she represents God and when she listens to him, he senses that God hears him as well.

At the close of the first session, Kevin notes that he feels that "God is with him" in what he is going through. "Not judging him, not saying much," but God is there just the same. Notice how different this is from his initial feeling that he is cursed by God.

God is, in fact, present in pastoral care conversations so that sense of being kept in mind flows actively from God's attentiveness to human suffering as it unfolds in the shape of a story. God pays attention to us and begins to mend our attachment needs in the intricate art of conversation.

Pastoral care conversations that help stories unfold are three-way conversations between the counselee, the pastor, and God, even if God is not mentioned. Wayne Oates, in his book *The Presence of God in Pastoral Counseling*, describes how important it is for ministers to imagine being Jesus, present for strength and sustenance as they counsel congregants.[9] "Bidden or not, God is there." This does not mean that ministers have a privileged communication with God, but that they remind people of how God is already faithfully present. When Pastor Janelle prays for Kevin between counseling sessions, she extends the sacredness of her care for Kevin further.

TIME

Setting apart a time for serious discussion helps people know that their story matters. Some people enter pastoral care with a great deal of distress. Time slips away from them helplessly. Ministers must make time sacred by setting aside special moments for conversation when they are asked for help.

When Kevin first sought Pastor Janelle, he sent her an email and asked to make an appointment with her to talk about a difficult period in his life. Because she was away on a retreat when the email first came, she responded to it three days later. She thanked him for reaching out and gave him a couple of options about when they could meet in her office. For safety reasons, she makes sure that there are other staff people in the office when they talk. At her desk she has a clock positioned so that she can see it, but Kevin cannot. By the end of forty-five minutes of conversation, she begins to bring the discussion to a close.

It is a good sign that Pastor Janelle was away on retreat when Kevin first emailed her. It means she is attending to her own needs for reflection and contemplation, a sacred gap in time for worship and prayer that helps her be available to those in her care. I will return to this subject in chapter 7. Nevertheless, her prompt response when she returns shows him that she cares enough about his story to give it the time it requires. Through the illusion of the hidden clock, she fosters an unhurried setting for Kevin to describe hidden parts of his story that touch on the past, present, and future. At the same time, not allowing the conversation to run more than an hour—while simultaneously not compulsively checking a watch—helps Kevin feel Pastor Janelle has time for his story and helps her to genuinely have the right amount of time.

In counseling, ministers talk about the past, present, and future, and thereby honor time. Kevin describes the fear he felt in his childhood home and explains how helpless he was when he was fired from his factory job. He talks about the hopeful and perplexing feeling of getting an education in the present. He thinks ahead to the future in which he can see himself doing something that he loves and that helps people—perhaps children or adolescents that felt worthless—to experience care. Because he gets a chance to tell his story with Pastor Janelle, he starts to put his past, present, and future into a framework that makes sense, developing a vision of how he might be of service to others.

Kevin expresses appreciation for Janelle's time. He tells her that he has not had the luxury of thinking about his life until he sat down in her office. He seems more restful after talking about his life with her and starts to find time again for things that had mattered to him in the past. Story care often slows people down enough to experience time that is honoring of their history.[10] This helps prepare them for a potential future. Pastoral conversation puts a break in time and sets it apart from ordinary experience.

Preserving the reverence of pastoral time also means setting boundaries. Kevin does not have access to Pastor Janelle's personal cell phone, and she responds to him with a work email during regular business hours rather than on her personal email. When she talks with Kevin, she tells him that if he has an emergency, he needs to call 9-1-1 or go to the emergency department. Otherwise, he can call the church office, leave a message, and she will get back to him the next day. This creates a set-apart time in which she can respond to his needs with some reflection.

CONTEXT

The first and most important context in this story is Kevin's family. Because she understands what is happening around them, Pastor Janelle puts Kevin's family story in a broader social framework. His family is just barely making it on their income, and they have less of a safety net to fall back on. In times of poverty when whole communities are in crisis, some families respond to such anxiety by turning inward. Kevin's father keeps rigid boundaries around his wife and children, controlling their time and dictating their activities. One of their family rules is not to speak to the outside world about what goes on in the family. Because she knows about his family background, Pastor Janelle says, "Thank you Kevin for coming to talk to me, because it must have taken some courage: you might be breaking the rule that says everything must stay in the family."

Events in the wider community impact families. Sometimes society presses on them.[11] Pastoral caregivers can resist these pressures by helping families meet their basic needs. For example, factory closures have led to a palpable despair.[12] High young adult unemployment puts young people like Kevin at risk for dangerous and self-destructive activities. This does not mean that society causes individual problems, but rather that people are always in relationship to their social world as well as their family.

Where you tell a story helps establish the narrative that is told. When a request is made for pastoral conversation, it is often helpful to have an office in which people can bring a sense of professionalism to the conversation. The context of a minister's office with religious memorabilia and art—frequently set in the context of a church—helps create a space for the elaboration of a new kind of story.

In this instance, Pastor Janelle's office gives Kevin the feeling that his story is taken seriously. Having conversations in a local restaurant or coffee shop may give mistaken feelings of familiarity between the minister and the congregant and thus may be inappropriate for the unfolding of difficult stories, so it should be avoided.

The region of the country in which someone's story is told may shape the content of the conversation and the rules by which it progresses. In some communities it is appropriate to give verbal affirmations and share similar experiences, offering a sense of kinship with the congregant's experience. In others it is better to provide a neutral holding space where the minister does not share her own story.

Through listening, Pastor Janelle expresses compassion because she sees how his relationship difficulties might reflect the social problems in their region. She understands the lack of opportunities available to Kevin and his peers in their part of the country. She wonders if other young people his age feel similar chronic disappointment. Although she understands these social factors, she does not explain the link she sees between the lack of financial opportunity and Kevin's despair. Instead, she listens carefully and connects with his human story. Compassion means listening without giving people the feeling that they are at fault.

The interwoven realities of family and social life are present in the hopes and fears of this specific time in a given setting. Putting a broad enough frame around a person's story makes it less likely that a minister will listen to a congregant as just *a problem person*, but rather they will attend to the influence a person's context has on the course of their problems.

MEANING-MAKING

Pastoral care for stories is complex work. When pastors listen to an individual's story, they listen with the ears and eyes of faith, seeking to help people make sense of their lives in a rich and nuanced fashion.

When Kevin tells his story to Pastor Janelle, he creates something new, a feeling that he is more than just a failure.[13]

Some people are driven by dominating narratives, and these are stories that define them.[14] Through meaning-making, careseekers can help them discover new stories about themselves. For example, Kevin thinks of himself as worthless because he feels powerless, and this makes him feel alone. Through talking with Janelle, he begins to see that he has taken important steps that show his own power.

One of the dominating narratives of the present time is the notion that *I am only valuable* if I can perform or succeed. Fearing failure, many people seek success as a form of self-definition to quell anxiety. People seek pastors because of a basic human need: the need for love and acceptance. They ask themselves, Will I be loved and accepted *by you* and *by God?* This basic question undergirds many pastoral conversations. If they live in a competitive culture, they may judge themselves as not measuring up.

When pastors listen, they begin to hear how people are more than their problems. This is one of the key gifts of the meaning-making that takes place in pastoral care conversations. Meaning-making involves discovering insight into one's story that puts it in a new light. This is only possible when one has attended to attachment, time, and context so that meaning starts to develop from one's story.

THE PASTOR'S FAITH AND HER OWN STORY

At times in ministry, it can be helpful to pause and reflect, "Why me, now?"[15] Pastor Janelle wonders, *Why has the person chosen me to receive a story?* She realizes that her only son has just gone off to college, leaving her family with an empty nest. She understands how hearing Kevin's story—a young man roughly the same age as her son—reminds her of her transition of losing a child to college, a loss that she had not openly discussed with her friends.

Pastor Janelle understands now how important it is for Kevin to reach out at this point in his life. Although she wishes she could have done more for him, she notes that he seemed to feel better because he talked to her. Pastor Janelle's ministerial imagination means that she sees Kevin as more than his problems and sees where he is already beginning to change.

Pastor Janelle understands the trust that Kevin placed in her and how she can carry this trust through faith. Holding this narrative in a compassionate manner is a significant intervention even though she wishes she could have done more to help him. Pastor Janelle's own faith is an important part of her intervention in pastoral care. Prayer, as a spiritual practice, is an active intervention in pastoral care, even if only done by the pastor in the privacy of her office.[16]

Prayer is one of the most important resources ministers have because it gives their work significance and helps lead to deeper insight. In the week between sessions, Pastor Janelle prays for Kevin. When she prays, she realizes that she had been worried for him, but she feels more peace through praying for him and his family. As she prays, she understands her own unresolved feelings about Kevin and his situation. Because she is attentive to the underdog in any situation, she realizes that her heart has been open to the pain that he was going through. Because of the way her heart is open, it is important that she has trust in God. She finds herself praying the psalms of lament on Kevin's behalf. As she prays for him, she realizes that he does not feel like a person of worth but that this does not match how God thinks of him. Instead, God thinks of Kevin as "the apple of [God's] eye" (Ps 17:8). Because of her prayer, Janelle feels peace that she has a key role in Kevin's story, and she understands now how Kevin sought her out for a reason and seemed to feel God's presence through their conversation.

Realizing that his story touched her heart for personal reasons, she almost wants to turn away from his grief. If she had trouble feeling God's faithful presence amid adversity, she wonders, *How could I share God's faithfulness with Kevin?* Because of her conversation with him, she begins seeing a spiritual director herself. To hear stories well, ministers need to have someone with whom they can share their own. By having someone who can listen to their own stories, ministers can feel grounded and thereby care for the stories of others.

For Pastor Janelle to help Kevin, it's important for her to discern her own purpose and vocation through the counseling relationship. Because he has less explicitly religious goals, she offers him three things to do before the next session that help him engage in life and expand his faith practices. He is to find one thing to do that makes him feel good about himself, he is to find one person to express gratitude toward, and he is to take one small move toward either a job or an educational opportunity. She also gives him the name of a local agency that is doing vocational support for people who have left the factory. Pastoral care begins with making a match, and it ends by offering some direction. Pastor Janelle realizes that she has established the kind of trust that makes it possible for her to make these suggestions to Kevin.

CONCLUSION

Once pastoral conversations had ended between Pastor Janelle and Kevin, his mother Pam began coming to church more regularly and taking communion, which she had never done in the past. Kevin continued to tend to the church garden until he got a job and moved away to another region, a choice that was made by many in his community.

When Pastor Janelle preached and prayed, she kept Kevin in mind, even though she did not continue to counsel him long-term. She thought about his distress, and she prayed that God's promises would be real to him. Kevin needed to know that God remembered him personally and loved him unconditionally despite all the ways that he did not feel like he measured up. Nevertheless, Pastor Janelle knew that her ministerial effectiveness would diminish if she tried to counsel him long-term. Through what she learned from him, she changed the church's programming, scheduling a family service of healing that included prayers and rituals for family support in challenging times.

In Pastor Janelle's conversation with Kevin, she did not need to mimic a professional counselor but rather be his minister. Although at the beginning his problems seemed poorly defined, she helped him feel understood and access the resource of his faith. Because of her knowledge of his family dynamics and her awareness of broader social factors, she was uniquely positioned to help him address the chief questions at this stage of his life, questions pertaining to dignity and vocation.

Through conversation, she helped him explore God's presence in his life and engage in the practice of gratitude. Pastor Janelle sought to express to Kevin that he is not worthless, and as a result, his faith began to change. Nevertheless, change in deep-seated stories does not happen overnight, so Kevin continued to struggles with a negative self-image and discouragement after his counseling sessions with her were finished.

To be effective, pastoral care conversation needs to address attachment, time, context, and meaning-making in a few sessions of counseling. The next several chapters describe specific scenarios of story care and how caring for these stories reflects God's faithfulness. Although these chapters address a set of different issues, they are united by the attempt to foster dignity and vocation in situations of despair and frustration.

The approach taken by a minister is fundamentally different from the problem-solving orientation of a psychotherapist: it is about offering a healing relationship that points people to God's presence. Ministers must be realistic that they cannot address all of people's problems in such conversations and accept that they can use their wisdom about psychological dynamics and social factors to enrich their own pastoral imagination, offering help at a key turning point in people's lives.

FOR FURTHER REFLECTION

1. Have you seen yourself meeting any of the needs for attachment, time, context, and meaning-making as you counsel people in your care? If so, how did these take shape?
2. How did Pastor Janelle care for her own story as she listened to Kevin's narrative? If you are a minister, do you have someone outside your congregation who hears your story?
3. What are some of the pastoral care needs in your context, and how are they similar to or different from the needs in Kevin's region?

2

FEELING REMEMBERED BY GOD

When Janine, a church deacon, goes to Margaret's house to visit, she is not sure what to do. She notices that Margaret lives in a messy house and that she can no longer manage the cleaning. Margaret complains about aging, but states that she feels most comfortable living in her own home. As Janine listens, the conversation deepens.

Janine realizes that Margaret's concern is existential. It is as if Margaret asks, "Do I matter anymore to the church, and to God?" When Margaret asks if she can bring her the Eucharist from the church, Janine says yes. After talking with her about what she needs, Janine asks if she can clean out her stove. As she does this activity, Janine feels centered and aware of herself, as if what she is doing comes from an attitude of prayer.

Margaret is honored by Janine's willingness to clean her stove and stunned by the sacrifice. Later, Janine goes to a deacons' meeting where a pastoral counselor from a local seminary was giving a talk entitled "How Not to Say the Wrong Thing." Janine tells the counselor what she has done for Margaret. The counselor objects, stating that it is boundary crossing.

Janine responds that her act of service was congruent with her identity as a minister and that her care came directly from the needs that Margaret had stated. Besides, it is only a matter of time before Janine herself will rely on a church deacon to help provide for her needs as she ages.

By listening to Margaret's story and responding with an act of service, Janine engaged in servant care that helped Margaret feel less lonely while also meeting some of Margaret's practical needs. Though it may look like ordinary service, a closer examination reveals the sacred elements of such service. Just as Peter refused when Jesus wanted to wash his feet (see John 13:7–8), many might initially refuse the deep care provided through acts of service. Many of the ministries of pastoral care, including listening, require the availability of the entire self with an attitude of service. One does not leave oneself behind to do such ministry. Instead, it requires engagement with one's entire self.

DEFINING MINISTRY

Ministry is the everyday activity of helping people know that God remembers them through service, compassion, and spiritual care. The calling involves the ordained service of teaching, preaching, and presiding at the sacraments offered by priests and clergy. It also includes the nuanced ministry of presence, listening, and advocacy that is also offered by chaplains and counselors.

Pastoral care remains close to the life of the church, its education and sacraments, whereas pastoral counseling brings the church's witness to life in the world. Pastoral care and counseling belongs on a continuum. Pastoral care is closer to the church with its sacramental identity. It tends to take stories at face value and involve short-term, sustained care. Pastoral counseling is a subspecialty that focuses on turning points, such as loss and grief, that occur in a person's life, and it usually takes place in the professional space of an office with a licensed and insured counselor. By caring for people at the crossroads, it helps persons discover how they are known and remembered by God as they discern life's purpose.

For Janine, being a servant minister to Margaret arose from her call established at baptism. In pastoral care and counseling, ministers of all types exercise their baptismal call to help people find their dignity and vocation.

Dignity is the belief that a person is created in the image of God with inherent worth, regardless of what that person can do or accomplish. As Laurence Holben says, "Every human person is, in and of him or herself, the whole, total, and complete focus of the self-emptying love that burns at the heart of God."[1] Pastoral care flows from the notion that each encounter with another person is an encounter with

17

God. This account of human dignity never diminishes, even if one loses important capabilities.

Vocation is the idea that a person is called to a distinctive purpose that may lie beyond their current horizon. In pastoral care, God's presence is implicit *exactly where people are.* God is also calling people to some greater purpose in their lives. No matter the obstacles in the way, God invests each life with a purpose beyond its own horizon. Regardless of one's capabilities, each person has something important to contribute to the ongoing creation of the world.

When ministers engage in pastoral care, they foster the dignity and vocation of the people they serve, thereby testifying implicitly to the self-giving care of Jesus Christ. Dignity and vocation are two sides of the same coin in pastoral care. Human dignity impels us to help people fully live their vocation; vocation affirms the inherent dignity already present in their God-given identity.

Although the previous vignette described a potentially humbling act when Janine cleaned the stove, she was fostering Margaret's dignity as a person who deserved a safe environment. Because Janine followed Margaret's lead and got her permission to care for her in this way, she reduced the potential for embarrassment. Janine sustained Margaret's vocation by helping her continue to live in a familiar setting, close to friends and supportive neighbors, for as long as possible. The entire conversation and action were undertaken with an attitude of respect.

The ministry of pastoral care and counseling has theological roots, not only secular ones, stemming from ancient religious ministry. Charles Gerkin argues that pastoral care reflects Hebrew ministry, the role of prophet—"confronting people with their deviation from the will of Yahweh," priest—"faithful and reverent observance of worship and cultic practices," and sage—"practical and moral guidance in the affairs of living together as a community."[2] Maintaining that pastoral care has been too closely identified with the sage, Gerkin declares that it is time to reclaim its prophetic and liturgical elements.

Janine's ministry with Margaret has elements of the ancient Hebrew roles of prophet, priest, and sage. When Janine listens to Margaret's story of aging, it is a prophetic task since elderly women are often invisible.[3] Margaret asks for the Eucharist to be brought to her, designating the priestly aspect of pastoral care. In helping her discern whether she can stay in the house, Janine is involved in the sage aspect of pastoral care.

Yet how can we classify the act of cleaning the oven? Gerkin's three categories do not directly address service as a form of pastoral care. Nevertheless, it resembles the foot-washing ministry of service in which Jesus washed his disciples' feet, an act that he defined as central to the formation of Christian ministry. By cleaning her oven, Janine added something significant, a component of service, to the ministry of pastoral care. At times, ministry includes meeting everyday needs. Servant ministry is an important aspect of pastoral care and counseling that is not directly addressed by the roles of priest, prophet, and sage, and it involves the willingness to receive help.

Orienting toward service relies upon a theological shift. A great deal of servant ministry sanctifies ordinary life as an arena where God is present. Following from a spirituality of the sacrament of everyday life, God often manifests under the veil of commonplace activities and events.

This means the ministry of pastoral care and counseling is sacred, even if it is a discussion of one's everyday life. Undertaken with an attitude of attention, servant ministry means asking someone about what they are going through, becoming aware of their needs, and responding with reverent action that takes their situation seriously. By asking for permission before acting, one avoids overstepping a boundary and doing something for someone that they do not need or appreciate. When servant-oriented pastoral care is effective, it often helps people slow down and appreciate the sacred presence of God in the mundane.

THE CONTEXTS OF PASTORAL CARE AND COUNSELING

There are three primary contexts in which pastoral care and counseling occur: the church, the hospital, and the counseling center. They are settings in which ministers foster the dignity and vocation of those whom they serve, attending to the mystery of everyday existence. Differing contexts require varying blends of the prophetic, priestly, sage, and servant roles. Pastoral care reflects God who, in love, founded the church for the purposes of confession, repentance, and healing of the world and creation. As a reflection of the church's ministry, pastoral care is part of God's purpose to heal the world, even when it does not always remain tethered to an explicitly Christian identity.

The primary context of pastoral care is the religious community and its life together. The form of pastoral care depends greatly upon the region and the ethnic setting in which it develops. In parishes, the goal is to sustain a community's identity so that they can return glory to God for all that God has done. Pastoral care, here, involves the exercise of the sacraments that meets individuals and families at each stage in their life journey and gives them strength and blessing at a turning point in their lives. Ministers who provide long-term care for a community in priestly or ordained roles seldom have time for in-depth pastoral counseling. Instead, they must meet short-term needs as they arise by focusing on ways to help people change and structure their communities so that the most people can have access to healing ministries. Additionally, ministers in religious communities often face multiple roles with the people for whom they provide pastoral care. At times they might counsel briefly before returning them to the pastoral care life of the community. Since they are involved in leading religious communities, the emotional dynamics can become complicated if they also provide in-depth pastoral counseling on a regular basis for those same persons with whom they lead in pastoral care scenarios.[4]

In pastoral care, caregivers in ministry, both ordained and lay, can network to destigmatize and normalize the suffering that a community is facing and provide education about it. Ordained ministers can play a crucial role in educating their communities about social issues and psychological problems, including addiction, mental illness, grief, dementia, and suicide, because of their proximity to these stories. Religious communities remain an underutilized source of healing and flourishing, especially in rural regions of the country.[5]

Ordained ministers play brief and essential roles in marriage preparation and couples counseling, fostering the growth of family systems. Pastoral care in religious communities requires balancing attention to the one who might have emotional problems and the life of the many. Often the best pastoral care arises from the church's organic attention to one another's suffering, such as in grief support groups.

In chaplaincy, the goal is to heal the caregiving community so they can continue ministries of compassion as a sign of love and justice. Chaplaincy began in hospitals that were extensions of the church's ministry of love and justice in the world. For ministers in hospital and hospice settings, physical and spiritual needs often overlap in care; people are often most vulnerable and aware of the ways they need to change in circumstances of illness and suffering. Care for sick individuals also becomes a time to care for the entire family system.

20

Chaplaincy in the hospital is more episodic; though in smaller communities, hospitals become centers of pastoral care for those who are frequently ill. Hospice chaplaincy becomes a way to accompany the terminally ill in a more intimate and intentional fashion. Ministry in mental hospitals becomes a sign of faithfulness to a God who seeks to relieve human anxiety and uplift the downtrodden. When ministers work in health care chaplaincy for an extended period of time, they often give pastoral care and counsel to the staff as much as the patients, and being a good chaplain requires engaging with the pastoral care needs of a burned-out medical community who often cannot express vulnerability as directly.

Pastoral counseling is a longer-term relationship with someone who seeks counsel about a particular problem or difficulty, and it takes place in an office for a set period of time. Pastoral counseling is the kind of disciplined attention that a caregiver gives when someone seeks their counsel. When counseling takes place, caregivers draw near to the deep needs and psychic longings in the human condition. Ideally, as in Pastor Janelle and Kevin's scenario described in the first chapter, pastoral counseling occurs in a set-apart time and place with a limited duration to address a pressing human concern. Those who seek a counselor are more troubled and may have part of themselves that wants to live and another part that wants to die. In pastoral counseling, the goal is to befriend and strengthen the part of a troubled person that wants to live.

Pastoral counseling is best performed by trained professionals who are licensed counselors working in stand-alone counseling centers where the counselors themselves receive ongoing supervision. Such counselors are also ordained ministers but are approved by their churches to represent the service of mercy in counseling. For ministers without counseling licenses, they are limited to a handful of such sessions before they are beyond their competency. Pastoral counseling is most effective when it is set apart from a person's life. When running into one's therapist in town, the client can decide whether or not to acknowledge the relationship. One may not have the same luxury with one's pastor or priest. Pastoral counseling needs to be a private relationship of trust where secrets can be borne.

Often the client in counseling heals through relationship by trading a particularly painful symptom for a relationship with a therapist.[6] At times, treatment can include developing relationships with the client's extended family to strengthen the communication of the family system. The theological purpose of the counseling relationship involves leading that individual to a deeper vocation, ameliorating symptoms so that a person can live more fully into the purposes God intends for their life. Each arena of pastoral care includes a vision of human dignity and vocation that emphasizes a different element of the prophet, priest, sage, and servant.

Pastoral ministry, whether lay or ordained, is a profound calling rather than a relationship of exchange. When Janine exercised care for Margaret, it reflected the church's ministry of mercy meant to alleviate suffering. It would still have been helpful to Margaret if Janine had cared for her as a paid employee, but the fact that she responded to her baptismal call by listening closely to her despair and cleaning her oven—with the parishioner's permission—meant that she worked as a witness of God's liberation through acts of service. Since all are relational creatures, the church requires acts of mercy to one another to fully live out it's calling.[7]

GIFTEDNESS FOR MINISTRY AND UNMET CHILDHOOD NEEDS

How did Janine become involved in the pastoral care ministry of the church? She was invited to do so by a group of parishioners who sensed her gifts for ministry, specifically that she was a compassionate person who noticed the suffering of others and asked them about it. One's gifts for ministry arise from a combination of God's calling, the community's recognition of that calling, the role one plays in one's family, and the early context as a child. Too much attention to any one factor leads to an imbalance in the calling and preparation for ministry.

Since the calling for ministry and the community's recognition of call is discussed elsewhere, this chapter focuses on the role one plays in one's family of origin and the early context of children's development as it impacts vocation.

As a middle child in her own family, Janine was skilled at mediating conflicts, an early learning that helped her navigate the inevitable disagreements arising in church ministry. At the parish, she noticed people's concerns and came armed with the right help and a directness and personal warmth that are a fitting combination to address many of the problems people face. Because of her family position, and some of the stresses her family faced as a child, she always felt most valuable when she was serving others.

For effective ministry to take place, it is also important to be aware of one's childhood needs and how they impact one's choice of vocation. Janine had to learn that she would naturally fall into a bridge-building role in her parish because of her sibling position as the middle child.

It was an asset in many circumstances, but it might not allow her to say the prophetic word necessary in other situations. For example, in some situations she sought to be the peacemaker or felt resentful if she was not heard and recognized. By becoming aware of one's own childhood roles and social contexts, a minister can more consciously engage in their reasons for doing ministry rather than being driven by unconscious ones that stem from one's family of origin and social context. Therefore, care for others' stories in pastoral care must begin with care for the minister's own stories. Here are a few examples:

> A gifted choral singer, a lay minister, leads the singing of psalms in her church because her mother sang to her as a child. She listens for the voice of God and, when she hears it, echoes it through her own.

> A minister in a minority context grew up watching his black father abused by the white community. His family was expected to "take" this abuse and not say anything about it. He used his childhood experience of the violence perpetrated against his own culture to advocate with whites in ways that led to transformation.[8]

> Another minister grew up in a Korean community where her church fulfilled a family function for a group that felt like "perpetual foreigners" in the larger society, even though they were the "model minority." Growing up in her community, she was expected to serve in associate positions and was treated more like a sister than a leader in a congregation because of her gender.[9] Although she felt her call was to become the senior pastor of a church, she struggled to establish her ministerial authority because of the ways women were seen. In response, she started a

support group for Asian women ministers, a group that assured each other a community of confidentiality.

A lay minister's father was involved in financial scandals as a board member of a parish. In adulthood, this man became a skilled accountant and began volunteering at his own parish. In his work there, he was extremely rigid and devoted time to double-checking the fiscal status of the church. While he earned a prominent position in the regional church's governing body, by going through spiritual direction he became aware of his father's powerful legacy and realized that his father's story was not necessarily his own.

One minister, who was a teenager when his father committed suicide, later became a minister with a highly positive outlook who avoided any hint of the negative. He disliked visiting elderly people who were sick. Instead, he focused many of the church's activities with the youth, always attempting to remain upbeat. Through a family systems presentation at his church, he became aware of the damage of unresolved loss in his own family and began to enter therapy with a counselor who understood suicide.

These examples describe one's childhood family system, social context, and individual psychology, and explain how each plays a role in developing the proclivity and gifts for ministry. It is important to emphasize that many of the examples include a real calling, a vocation that comes out of the intersection of one's joy and the world's deep need. Nevertheless, if ministers are not aware of the unconscious elements involved in their own calling, they may become less effective as their own childhood needs remain unmet and can burn out altogether. Unmet childhood needs are an important part of the vocation to ministry.

An unconscious hurt diminishes much of the joy of the calling of ministry. Alice Miller describes therapists as being motivated by unconscious needs from childhood that put the emotional lives of others before their own.[10] Something similar may happen to ministers. Engaging in ministry driven by unconscious childhood needs can lack joy and a centered calm, and may lead to the twin problems of contempt for others and acting out in self-destructive ways. If childhood needs are never met, ministers may go looking for church contexts and chaplaincy settings that confirm their worthiness, risking boundary violations in the process.

While the impulse to do ministry comes out of God's call and the needs of the church, the experience of one's childhood predisposes one to certain types of ministry. People who cared for their caregivers in their families of origin may be gifted listeners and intuitively pick up on psychic pain in a person and an organization. Those who faced silenced grief may lose awareness of the impact of grief in their own story, becoming somewhat aloof to the people whom they serve.

When a minister can come to understand the unconscious elements of their own lives, they can allow God to transform childhood needs into gifts that can be used for service to others; signs of healing and growth. Often this requires having a counselor or spiritual director who listens to the minister attempting the demanding work of pastoral care. With the proper support, what might have begun as a painful incident of unmet needs becomes an opportunity for the Spirit to enable pastoral care to happen, just as through the experience of prolonged grief one can sometimes experience God's grace given back into one's life as one receives the "desires of one's heart," if only in a veiled form.[11] The desires of one's heart are a combination of the unconscious impulses from the past and the intentions that God places in the human spirit for the future.

Unconscious reasons for entering ministry are only one part of the constellation of God's call on a person's life, and God can use these unconscious needs to lead to deeper ministry once they are brought to the level of consciousness. Paradoxically, unmet childhood needs are not only the kernel of the gifts of ministry for each person, but some aspects of these needs must also be met in personal relationships outside of work for ministers to care in responsible ways.

For ministers to care for the stories of others in parishes, hospitals, and counseling centers, they must first feel remembered by God, even in their unconscious selves. The feeling of being remembered by God must be present not only in the public self that they present to others, but also in the hidden private self, with its dreams and unconscious wishes. Understanding that their hidden self is accepted by God prepares them to take risks and engage in emotionally free ministry.

Being accepted by God beyond any shadow of doubt is the conceptual and emotional core of effective pastoral care ministry. Therefore, self-care is an essential element of all pastoral care and counseling. By exploring the private world of complex motivations, ministers can know that their story is remembered, even if they felt that their unmet childhood needs rendered them unlovable to God. Rather than defending themselves against their own vulnerability by becoming "perfect" in the quest to please others, ministers can feel remembered in their own neediness, that unavoidable form of vulnerability that is part of the human condition.

LAMENT AND MEMORY

Pastoral care is an act of keeping someone in mind that helps a person feel meaningful to God. As an example, remembering a name or a personal situation or sending a condolence card creates the conditions of feeling remembered. Such care begins with having the soul "minded" by God. According to James Ashbrook, minding includes "tending, taking care of, watching over, and feeling concern about."[12] When we remember others, we actively help them create a healthy sense of self, which is fundamentally rooted in the fact of being known and loved by God. Pastoral care expresses healthy selfhood by keeping others in mind. What follows is a description of how memory works in pastoral care that explains connections to trauma studies and recent theological approaches to memory. God's memory leads to liberation from oppression and fosters the capacity to lament, thus creating the sense of Christ's presence.

There are indications that this process of "minding" others has tremendous potential to contribute to psychological healing, even among the most traumatized. Trauma theorist Jon Allen has defined this as "mentalizing," or "awareness of mental states and processes in oneself and other persons."[13]

Bessel van der Kolk describes being kept in mind by others as the heart of good trauma treatment, no matter the modality. His notions pertain because many of the situations ministers face in pastoral care can be defined as traumatic. "Being truly heard and seen by the people around us, feeling that we are held in someone else's mind and heart," is a powerful experience.[14] He further defines the vivifying effect of such attention. "As long as we feel safely held in the hearts and minds of the people who love us, we will climb mountains and cross deserts and stay up all night to finish projects."[15] Even in situations where people have not faced trauma, careseekers benefit from ministers who can remember them and their stories. Pastoral care and counseling works by keeping others in mind, which creates a self by establishing safety and narrative coherence out of fragmented experience. As spiritual caregivers, ministers often help people feel that God keeps them in mind.

Pastoral care is not a two-way relationship between a healer and a patient, but a three-way relationship that includes God as the primary agent who heals. As noted in the previous chapter, because God listens actively to the caregiver's own stories of suffering and despair, ministers can then begin to keep in mind those for whom they care. When people are understood by a pastoral caregiver, they can more easily come to depend on God for nurturance and direction.

By developing the ability to listen carefully to what another says in comfortable silence, pastoral caregivers can reflect the theological notion that we are known and loved by a provident God, that what we are doing in pastoral care is enough. The conviction that God listens to us in our suffering is the most important aspect of pastoral care, as it provides the foundation for a deep sense of trust, which we saw in Pastor Janelle's attachment to Kevin in the introduction.

Yet pastoral memory is not simply about feeling better. It also unleashes painful memories that cry out for lament and demand justice. The memory of God is also a political force that leads to the freedom of slaves and the unbinding of those who are oppressed. Drawing from the exodus narratives and the notion of covenant, John Patton describes how being remembered by God led the Israelites out from a situation of slavery and unjust treatment into a new home and a sense of covenant community.[16] God's faithful memory holds the limited and fragile memory of believers, especially those who have been enslaved and oppressed, creating a caring community. God's memory of the oppressed keeps them in mind and leads to freedom. Pastoral care requires a prophetic approach and a compassionate response. The two go together.

Even in the most extreme situations, God's memory of us is an important source of comfort and justice, and it redefines notions of personhood. God's memory becomes most significant when our own

memory fails. For example, people lose their identity through dementia and need a community that can remember them for more than
their disease.[17] John Swinton argues that our society has a limited concept of what it means to be human, based on hypercognition and ratio-
nality. As pastoral caregivers, we need to describe a Christian form of
memory that is rooted in the promise of the resurrection, in which
we can remember those who no longer remember themselves.[18] God
holds us in memory; we do not depend upon our worth to the social
community as a measuring stick of our worth before God.

Many of the scenarios in which pastoral care is needed are situations of suffering. God's memory includes lament, so it is not necessary
to "change the subject" when we encounter conditions of suffering.
Lament is an oft misunderstood word. It means crying out to God,
but it also includes a demand that injustice be alleviated. When God
remembers us, it is not so that we can cope better or adjust to circumstances of suffering, but rather so that the unnecessary sources of suffering can be changed.

Lament is not quietistic, but leads directly to prophetic action.
The kind of memory that includes lament awakens the call for justice. According to Johannes Baptist Metz, a political theologian who
reflected on the Holocaust, all too often people remember with rose-
colored glasses to ignore violence. Because, in the act of his own sacrifice, Jesus Christ transformed suffering, memory does not need to
shy away from lament. Instead, pastoral caregivers can address it more
directly, transforming it by attending to it. Jesus Christ's suffering is
present when we suffer, connecting us to God through the experience
while at the same time delegitimating unjust suffering resulting from
oppression.

Questions of memory and lament are important even in quotid-
ian acts of care, such as the service provided to Margaret by Janine at
the beginning of this chapter. Margaret thought of aging as a form of
suffering and described it as such. Janine wanted to validate her experience even though she had not gone through it herself. She also won-
dered if she should change the subject and try to improve Margaret's
mood instead of dwelling on the negative.

Resisting her temptation to encourage, she listened and began
to understand Margaret's testimony as a form of lament. Janine was
positioned as a witness to her sorrow. She pictured herself as a psalmist directing complaints to God as Margaret talked. When Margaret

asked, "Where is God?" in her struggles of aging, she asked the question of theodicy—the question of how God could allow bad things to happen to good people. Janine did not answer Margaret's question but prayed silently to herself as she listened. Lament is one of the chief ways that pastoral caregivers can point to the tenderness and mercies of God.

Staying with Margaret in the pain of what she is going through, Janine used her attention to deepen the memory of suffering, and this helped her bring to life the transforming power of Jesus Christ's own death and resurrection through the act of remembrance without feeling like she needed to answer Janine's questions. The theodicy question is a perennial one, and pastoral care does not need to answer it, but rather, to give this question the space to be asked repeatedly. As Metz states,

> Of course theology, as far as I can see, cannot "solve" this theodicy question. Its task rather consists in this: to allow the question to be asked again and again, to make it clear that the question cannot be transferred to human jurisdiction, and to work out the concept of a temporally charged expectation that *God*, in God's own time, will justify himself [*sic*] in the face of this history of suffering.[19]

Janine's open-ended, reflective, and sacred listening to Margaret as she shared lament-filled stories of aging helped Margaret to voice her pain rather than silence it. To do this effectively, a minister does not have to have answers to suffering but rather keep faith with the memory of it.

For ministers to care for painful memories and not become discouraged, it is necessary to direct the pain of lament to God, thereby keeping faith with the sorrow of memory. This means keeping their own faith that is grounded in the trust that ultimate justice will come from God. Just as attachment keeps us in mind, lament-filled questions bring the suffering of life to God's attention through the form of testimony. While care does not always involve fixing the suffering, it does require attention to God's presence amid suffering.

When pastoral caregivers listen to others, even in secular settings, they implicitly bear witness to Jesus Christ, who authorizes their ministry. Wayne Oates reminds readers that Christ is present when two or more are gathered in his name, and everyday pastoral caregivers work in Christ's presence. Simply being a minister, a representative of a religious institution as an ordained or nonordained pastoral counselor, or a hospice chaplain, institutes this presence. When caregivers listen to stories, they do not need to feel that they must add Jesus to the conversation. Jesus is always present as the conversation takes place. When ministers and counselors remember that God is present with them in the act of listening, they can feel God's care even as they try to keep faith with difficult memories. The memory of God unfailingly occurs in this presence, creating situations of liberation, even as caregivers listen.

THE HEART OF PASTORAL CARE

Traditionally, pastoral care has drawn heavily from the social sciences, including listening skills and psychotherapeutic intervention to human problems. In recent years, social service work has come under the mandate of managed care to create behavioral treatments that address measurable psychosocial goals. Some pastoral theologians have started to engage this literature for pastoral care. Recent innovations in counseling and clinical practice have shifted the field's attention to best practices and measurable outcomes. While much good has come from the literature's attention to science, and new legitimacy has come to the field of pastoral care in a medical sense, something has sometimes been ignored—the tone of pastoral care.

The tone of pastoral care is slowing down, attending, and remaining present along the way, rather than filling in a chart and rushing people out the door. Through good pastoral care, people often find themselves slowing down and savoring life more than they did before. The outcome of pastoral care as a contemplative practice is the ability to look deeply into the questions of purpose in one's life. This capacity is bound up in the contemplative frame in which pastoral care takes place. Counselors and ministers, however, are beginning to reclaim some of the treasures of the contemplative tradition for a new generation.

In the ministry of pastoral care, the approach is contemplative rather than problem focused. In maintaining that pastoral care is first and foremost a spiritual discipline—undergirded by prayer—in which persons discern God's presence in life's difficulties, the shift occurs between the means tested and the mystical.

Pastoral care is an ordinary gift of listening to another with depth. Brother Lawrence described going through periods of despair and doubting his faith until he developed an ability to tend to God's presence in his everyday life.[20] Jean-Pierre de Caussade argued that everyday activities provide a window into the attention required from the spiritual life.[21] These mystics remind caregivers that it is possible to discern God's presence in the ordinary events of everyday listening when proper spiritual attention is given to them.

To return to the case example from the beginning, when Janine met Margaret and heard her story, she was meeting a person in whom burned the image of God, a person with dignity and vocation. As she heard Margaret's story of aging and feeling invisible in the process, she felt God's presence in the telling of the story. This did not come as comfort or consolation. It did not change the subject from the narrative of suffering and invisibility. Rather, it assured Janine of God's faithful and steadfast presence in Margaret's life. In that simple act of Janine getting down and cleaning Margaret's stove, Janine felt the sustenance of God's presence. It was as if, in the ordinary act of service, God's presence became known through gentle, sustained attention.

FOR FURTHER CONSIDERATION

1. How have you seen the prophetic and liturgical element of pastoral care at work?
2. Is your own ministry closer to pastoral care or counseling? How could you tell the difference or how do you know when you are switching roles?
3. Following the theology of lament outlined in this chapter, why is it not important to try to "cheer someone up" in pastoral care?

3

STORIES OF SUICIDE SURVIVORS

Pastoral ministry is a daily encounter with difficult grief. This story, placed so early in the book, shows how pastoral care requires courageous ministerial imagination. The scenario illustrates how to help people find hope in situations of profound grief, noting that pastoral care points to God who is the ultimate reason for hope. Suicide survivors may want to read through this chapter slowly, making sure they have supportive people they can talk with about their experience as they proceed.

Fifteen-year-old Jeremy shoots himself with a gun in the basement of his home. He has just gone through a romantic breakup and states in the suicide note that he "does not have the strength to go on." Jeremy has become isolated from many of his friends and even his mother, June. He has withdrawn from familiar parish activities. His father, Ralph, finds Jeremy and, in addition to calling the police, calls their trusted priest.

What is the ministerial response to suicide, and how does it reflect God remembering us in life's most challenging times? Putting his other plans at the parish aside, Father Bill stays with Ralph and June throughout the entire day and helps them arrange funeral services. As soon as the police come and take away Jeremy's body for an autopsy, they cry out to God in despair. Father Bill realizes the importance of his role at that time, staying with them in silent prayer and holding their grief.

As their parish priest for five years, he has provided care as their faith is growing; now he witnesses through loss, providing care in extremity. By being with them through this time, he expresses God's presence to them. Suicide loss incites incredible initial pain and long-term despair, creating a crisis of meaning in which a person's story falls apart. Ministers can play a distinctive role in helping families remember their loved one and reconstruct their image of God after loss. The last chapter explained the activity of pastoral care as lament in which one does not have to cheer the other person up; this chapter extends this thought into a practical situation faced by far too many families.

Amid his overwhelming schedule, Father Bill tries to find time to meet with Ralph and June to talk. In talking with them, he hopes to keep faith with their memories of suffering. After talking for three hours, he goes home exhausted. "Do I have what it takes to minister to this family?" Father Bill asks himself. "How do I continue to hope amid this struggle?" Bill wonders to himself. "What is Jesus trying to say to me through this story?" These questions are answered by attention to ministry immediately after suicide, a discussion of the important emotional and spiritual processes that occur through suicide, and a discussion of longer-term responses to suicide loss. Because of Father Bill's faith, he can accompany Ralph and June with less anxiety himself. Having cried out to God in his own crises, he can walk with them in their journey. Yet regardless, he senses his inadequacy for the task.

MINISTRY IMMEDIATELY AFTER SUICIDE

Before the funeral, Father Bill gathers June, Ralph, and their chosen family members to tell stories about Jeremy. "How did God let this happen?" they ask. "How could Jeremy leave us behind?" "What signs did we miss?" Father Bill listens attentively but does not answer their questions. Instead, he makes space for them to be voiced. He understands the pastoral maxim, *"the greater the crisis, the fewer the words."*[1] Father Bill asks them directly if they want him to acknowledge that Jeremy died by suicide in the funeral homily. They say they do since it is already news around the community. If they had insisted that Jeremy's death was an accident, he would have accepted this answer too, as he slowly works with them to help them face the tragic death. He has been careful to proceed according to the family's wishes.

Preaching the funeral, Father Bill acknowledges Jeremy's suicide as an act of intolerable pain, and his sermon focuses on other stories of his life, insisting that his suicide does not define Jeremy's story. In the process, he also discourages "copycats" who might be drawn to follow down Jeremy's path.[2]

Father Bill also needs to manage the parish's care for the family. In the week following the suicide, one of the church deacons tells June that Jeremy has committed a grave affront against God. Father Bill explains to June and Ralph that the deacon is mistaken. He believes that God does not hold people responsible for situations of intolerable pain and that everyone has suffered enough. The primary meaning that Father Bill wants to convey is that God is compassionate. Pastorally he hopes to listen to June and Ralph's suffering, to hear their pain, and so witness God's action in the world. He believes that God is with the family. Through his ministering, he wants to increase the family's capacity for hope without saying anything condescending or paternalistic.

Father Bill is in a meaning-making emergency that requires all the resources of compassion and faithful witness. Paradoxically, the right response in such a situation is few words, supportive presence, and an attitude of "not knowing" what the other person is going through by which one communicates that at the same time one wishes to know.[3]

CULTIVATING ATTACHMENT, TIME, CONTEXT, AND MEANING-MAKING

Families respond to suicide in a range of ways, some never speaking of it at all. Yet each family is transformed by it.[4] Suicide survivors often feel lost and alone. Ministers are not experts in relationship to this kind of story, but they are able to listen compassionately to a situation of unbearable pain. In the first chapter, it was argued that story care was effective by attending to attachment, time, context, and meaning-making. Each of these areas is essential to responding wisely to stigmatized suicide loss.

Attachment. When people experience a traumatic loss such as suicide, they may feel grief, resentment, and self-blame. They may wonder how their bonds with their loved ones could be so deeply fractured. Ministers make a difference in such situations by letting them express grief and fear so that they can attach to their ministers.

Attachment can begin to heal by a minister's attentive care. Suicide survivors frequently appreciate and benefit from long-term pastoral care, whether through visitation, phone calls, or cards. Father Bill is diligent about visiting June and Ralph every couple of months. Once, when he visits June and Ralph for dinner in their home, he notices June placing a table setting at Jeremy's spot at the table even though it had been three months since the loss. She breaks down in tears when she realizes her mistake. Father Bill witnesses this despair: he is responsible to be compassionate and see the suffering as it happens. He replies, "I have no idea what you're going through, but it must be so hard." Acknowledging her suffering and wanting to understand, he shows the hallmark of an empathic pastoral response, which is different from feeling the same feelings as the person suffering. Empathy requires not knowing what another is going through and is a crucial component in attachment.

Time. Through suicide, time is literally stolen from families. Survivors might feel haunted by the memory of the suicide as time keeps looping back to the event. Suicide loss is a traumatic bereavement, a death that, witnessed or not, is particularly violent and unusual. Such a bereavement interferes with time.[5] Losses like this frequently create post-traumatic stress disorder (PTSD) among survivors, frequently lasting more than a year.[6] After suicide, survivors relive a scene in their minds in flashbacks, are easily startled, or go numb and lose touch with their bodies. All these responses demonstrate the deep fragmentation they have endured.

By listening to the rupture of suicide grief, ministers help people reconfigure their relationships with time, helping it to become sacred again. In the first couple of months after she lost Jeremy, June felt disconnected from her body and wandered around the house. Ralph was mostly quiet, but he did admit to drinking more. All such reactions are common after traumatic bereavement, and these reactions are an attempt to deal with the disruption of time.

June and Ralph need professional therapists who are also bereavement counselors. They *also* need a minister whose attentive responses point them to God's ongoing presence. Ministry with suicide survivors means long-term accompaniment. Father Bill continues to write them condolence cards on important anniversaries (six months, one year, two years) and makes pastoral visits to their home. In this way, fragmented time begins to be restored through being remembered. When suicide survivors feel remembered by their ministers, it helps them feel remembered by God.

Context. Pastoral care for suicide survivors must consider the actual physical setting of the suicide as well as cultural and social aspects of this loss. Father Bill is aware that since the suicide happened in the home, they may need help to redeem space from the traumatic memory.

Social factors such as unemployment, inadequate health care, or a recent diagnosis sometimes increases the risks for suicide and, thus, community-wide stress can be a contributing factor. By understanding the context, a minister responds with more compassion and less blame. Jeremy's group of adolescent peers could have been a small-group context where suicide was glorified. All these contextual factors can heighten suicide risk.

Meaning-making. Suicide is a lonely grief. *Why did my loved one die and leave me behind? Why is everyone now afraid to talk to me about him?* These are the kinds of questions that haunt survivors. Expressing such questions can help survivors put the pieces of their lives back together. Because suicide loss is stigmatized, survivors often face *disenfranchised grief,* a grief that is silenced because it is not seen as normal or because nobody recognizes it.[7] When a grief is disenfranchised, it can interfere with healing because it cannot come into the open. Ministers can normalize such a loss by confirming this loneliness, saying that they are not at fault for surviving another's suicide, mentioning the loved one in conversation, and stating that the process of grieving takes longer than most people think.

Survivors know that their loved one was more than "a suicide," but they may worry that the deceased will only be remembered through the lens of their final, seemingly desperate act. Ministers can help people grieve by inviting loved ones to tell richer stories about the deceased.

When he visits them for the second time, Father Bill asks the following question: "Would it be OK with you if I asked you about some things that I did not know about him? I've noticed that sometimes suicide survivors want their loved ones to be remembered for more than just the cause of their death."[8] Ralph and June respond with relief after this question is asked and pull down the family albums and talk for hours. They seem to welcome the invitation to tell more stories about their beloved son.

DUAL-PROCESS MODEL OF CARING

Because suicide is a traumatic bereavement, people need specific aftercare that addresses their grief process and the memory of the deceased. When Father Bill visits, he asks two kinds of questions, called the dual-process model of coping with grief, an approach to traumatic grief counseling that helps establish safety and make meaning.[9]

The first set of questions is about *how survivors are functioning* in their daily lives. *Are Ralph and June able to manage their daily affairs?* Father Bill wonders and finds ways to ask about this. June returns to work after a month off. Their house is beginning to feel put together again after several months of being in disarray, and Ralph does most of the cleaning. Paying attention to the daily functioning of each family member after loss is important; sometimes people cannot take care of themselves after traumatic bereavement.

The second set of questions explores the ongoing relationship with the deceased, whether in memories, dreams, visions, or a felt presence. Called *continuing bonds*, these can create a new sense of purpose or help people feel that they are not entirely alone. Sometimes people even choose to dedicate some part of their lives to the deceased.[10]

Father Bill says, "Sometimes people find special ways to remember the deceased or, this might strike you as somewhat strange, communicate with them. What kind of special relationship do you hope to have with Jeremy and how will you connect with his memory? Are there any places where you feel his presence?"[11]

Suicide survivors often want to continue their relationship with the deceased but may have complicated feelings that interfere with the ability to do so. They may feel guilt at continuing with life after their loved one is gone, anger at their perception that their loved one was being selfish, and regret that they had not alleviated the problem.

Right after suicide, people are often besieged by memories. Such mixed emotions can take over. After some months, they need ways to cultivate painful memories, even stewarding them as a sign of faithfulness.[12] At times, they also need permission to let the painful memories go. When Father Bill asks if they ever felt Jeremy's presence after his death, June says that occasionally she dreams that Jeremy opens a door and wordlessly beckons to her, but she finds herself frozen in place.

When Father Bill asks Ralph about whether he ever feels Jeremy's presence, Ralph shows him a memorial he created to his son's memory in the shed, a place where they used to work on projects together. When visiting the memorial or going fishing on a special stretch of their favorite river, Ralph feels Jeremy's presence in a tangible and pleasant way. Sensing this was important, Father Bill encourages Ralph to continue such practices. Amid unbearable grief, people often make rituals to remember those they have loved or choose ritual objects that link them to the loved one.

After traumatic bereavement, survivors may unconsciously keep things the same to preserve the memory of their loved one. This is a veiled form of continuing bonds expressed through the beloved object or place. By choosing a few special objects that have ongoing meaning to them related to the loss, they have receptacles of sacred treasure that stand for the person's presence.

Memorializing the past is normal. Yet, after several years, preserving everything in the exact fashion can begin to shade into complicated grief, which is a grief that has been frozen and cannot move forward.[13] At times, families euphemize suicide loss, fabricating stories about what happened rather than facing the loss.[14] In these instances, in addition to the help of trained counselors, families need ministers who can gently and lovingly face the suicide with them in order to heal. By using compassion and pastoral imagination, ministers responding to suicide can engender hope and authentic grieving by helping loved ones face the loss. In helping the lament to happen, they are keeping faith with the memory of loss, one of the most sacred tasks of Christian practice.

After a traumatic loss, it is also normal to experience sleep disruption, stomach pain, dejection, fits of rage, nightmares, headaches, and increased use of alcohol or other substances. If the bereaved continue to experience disruption in their sleep or daily routines six months after a traumatic loss, they may need the ongoing support of a professional bereavement counselor. Suicide support groups help survivors remember long after others seem to have forgotten and moved on or simply feel too uncomfortable about the loss to bring it up.

FAITH AFTER LOSS

For Christians, traumatic bereavement can disrupt their explicit connection to God. It may be harder for them to pray, sing, take the sacrament, and serve since everything they believe in has been thrown into question through the loss. The fact that people seem to have their beliefs shaken after suicide is no surprise, and ministers can be sensitive to this response as another part of the grief. Grief can disrupt one's taken-for-granted faith. Ministers are aware of how expressing loss before God—like the lament of the prophets—is a faithful form of worship.[15] Likewise, expressing the grief of lament over suicide is a transformative aspect of Christian worship.

In the months after Jeremy's death, June and her husband Ralph slowly stop coming to the parish. June states that she "lost her faith" because of Jeremy's suicide. Before Jeremy died, June says she believed in a loving and personal God who was moved to action by prayer. Now she feels as if God has betrayed her. Prayer has gone from being a vital exercise to one that feels empty.

Like many others who find themselves with a new identity after the suicide of a family member, Ralph and June lose the signposts of their familiar lives. So many of the promises of faith no longer make sense to them.[16] Well-meaning parishioners say, "God never gives you more than you could handle," or "God needs a little angel and took Jeremy," which Father Bill suggests says more about the parishioner's anxiety than the rich tradition of faith. After the funeral, the couple mostly feels forgotten because they sense the parish does not know how to talk to them.

June and Ralph no longer feel connected to God because of their grief. It is not simply a *dark night of the soul*; it feels like the death of God. Rather than trying to talk them back into faith, Father Bill accompanies them through their time of personal darkness, attempting to witness as faithfully as possible to their experience, believing that this emptiness is precisely where God is found.

Father Bill shows them love rather than telling them that God loves them. Thus the old writing adage, *Show, don't tell*. He does so by accepting their questions and not seeking to give them answers. He also goes to a spiritual director himself, knowing that it is important to care for his own story so that he can care for their painful narrative. He realizes that being angry with God is normal and allows them space for this anger. If he did not have a space to discuss his grief, he could feel overwhelmed in this care.

Father Bill counsels June and Ralph for several months, during which he focuses on their biggest theological questions rather than shying away from them. He finds that their minds, lives, and faith have been deeply shaped by loss. This is not a "bump in the road" that they are going to get over quickly. What is essential for their recovery is an extended period of lament uninterrupted by attempts to cheer them up.

Traumatic bereavement is an interruption to life's story. Interruptions in one's life story are also interruptions in one's relationship with God. Ralph and June ask their poignant questions of Father Bill, stating, "How did God let this happen?" "Have I failed as a parent?" and "Why am I here while he is gone?" just like they did at the funeral, but now six months later. Ministers should not think they must answer these questions, but rather create a space for them to be asked, because God is present in the asking. It is fine to say, "I don't know the answer to that question, but I'd like to explore what it means for you."

As we discussed in the previous chapter, Johann Baptist Metz, a German theologian who wrote extensively about the Holocaust, noted that it was not important to answer the question about where God was in suffering, but rather to allow space for that question to be asked over and over again.[17] Theologically, lament helps us see that crying out to God is also a form of worship. It is one of the chief ways that caregivers witness to the tenderness of God. All too often, ministers believe they need to answer questions, but pastoral care for suicide survivors means allowing space for lament. Crying out to God in deep trauma is, in fact, an act of faith.

THE IMAGE OF GOD

Faith is the expression of one's deepest longings, the distinctive outline of the desire for God that creates the boundaries of one's life story.[18] The shape of faith changes across the lifespan. Pastoral care's primary aim is to help people meet the true and living God when they experience profound disruption.

Everyone has at least two understandings of God, conceptual and experiential. The conceptual understanding can be stated out loud when asked; the experiential is felt without needing to say anything. Traumatic loss impacts both understandings. A conceptual understanding of God could be put into a catechetical response. An experiential understanding of God is visceral, expressed by crying out, journaling, or interpersonal sharing.[19] It is felt when God's presence is experienced as a soothing, comforting parent or a familiar childhood song.

Our experiential understanding of God is related to our relationship with early attachment figures.[20] As we are raised, our family imprints on us early experiences of care and nurture, and we are surrounded by a culture that gives us images that help us feel that we belong and are worthwhile. Otherwise we feel that our environment is insecure.

June was raised in an environment with a clear message that you must take care of yourself. This impacted her conceptual understanding of God so that when she became a Christian, she held a firm belief that God was in control of her life.

Ralph was raised in a controlling situation where he was expected to succeed, but faith did not seem to be the center of his experiences. When he became a Christian, he found hope in a God who gave him the space that he needed to live out his faith. Ralph described to Father Bill how God created a "fence" around his life that gave him the freedom to be who he needed to be. This was paradoxical since the fence gave him both freedom and boundaries. In these statements June and Ralph describe their experiential understandings of God as they relate to early attachments, reflecting on how they shaped their conceptual understandings of God.

Seeking to raise their son in faith, the couple returned to the parish as young people. In addition to experiencing the deep worship of the parish, the central message they got from the priest's homilies was that God was with them in the good and bad times of their lives. This helped them deepen their faith and prepare for loss. Before the suicide, they were involved in a small-group Bible study of young families at their parish and appreciated becoming friends with other Christians.

When Jeremy died, June faced deep contradiction. She had thought God only loved her if God controlled her life. Now everything was out of control. Ralph felt that all his freedom was taken away now that Jeremy was gone. The fences that gave him boundaries and made sense out of his life were broken down. Conceptual understandings of God were shattered.

Both June and Ralph felt God's experiential presence by singing "Here I am, Lord" at the funeral and praying the Lord's Prayer at the internment. The experiential knowledge of God was like a security blanket for both. Experiential understandings of God help suffering people make it through challenging times. The conceptual and experiential understandings of faith come together in the church's practices of worship and prayer.

As he talks to June and Ralph, Father Bill wonders about their conceptual and experiential understandings of God. "What are some things you believed about God before Jeremy died and how have they changed? What have you done and what has God done for you to make it through this time?"

In the conversation he found that God indeed was not dead to them, but their conceptual understanding of God was changing rapidly and their experience of God's presence was being felt less often. In a time of rapid transitions, when the story of life is shifting, sometimes the old narratives make little sense. He also asked them about their experiential understanding, "When have you experienced a comforting presence or had a feeling that everything was going to be all right?" These questions, asked with sensitivity during counseling sessions, can help express the deep longings that shape life.

HELD IN THE MEMORY OF GOD

Safe conversation in which people feel kept in mind by others helps them feel kept in mind by God. In the previous chapter, we saw how Bessel van der Kolk defined being "kept in mind" as being at the heart of trauma therapy. Likewise, effective pastoral care and counseling helps people feel kept in mind by the church and God. Alternatively, dis-membered people can lose track of both physical and mental continuity.

Being held in someone's mind and heart is the core of pastoral ministry.

As Father Bill sends June and Ralph condolence cards, mentions Jeremy's name—with their permission—in the All Saints' Day service, and visits them on the six- and twelve-month anniversaries of the loss, he keeps them in mind and helps them feel that God remembers them. Father Bill participates in the gracious nature of God's memory as he listens to Ralph and June and does not try to solve their difficulties.

When the priest approaches a human life story with its hopes and ambitions as well as its distinctive joys and pains, he helps careseekers experience how their *unique* human life is remembered by God. Secular counseling allows a person to express their thoughts, attitudes, and ideas, but pastoral counseling directs those thoughts, attitudes, and ideas to God, believing that God accompanies the counselor each step of the way.

Counseling is like a prayer since a minister can be praying silently for the person who is sharing his or her story. At the same time, God listens to pastoral counseling, accompanying it along the way. Pastoral care can occur without naming God. Bidden or not, God is present.

When a minister hears a person's story, a minister listens to a communal narrative of God's care implicit in that story. Accompaniment through "the valley of the shadow of death" echoes God's faithfulness to God's people in both collective and personal dimensions. This collective relationship involves identifying with the suffering of people in slavery (see Exod 2:23–25). Scripture often invites readers to remember the poor who are being treated without dignity based on the conviction that God remembers them (see Ps 41:1). Yet Scripture also has a personal dimension, reminding believers of God's faithfulness through suffering and giving us the sense that God remembers believers as individuals amid this suffering.

In the case of Father Bill's care for June and Ralph, it is not necessary that they verbally assent to any proposition about God to show their faith. As they experience God's absence, Bill listens to them struggle without needing to provide answers. Letting people voice their lament in pastoral care does not have to lead them out of the suffering. Henri Nouwen suggests that instead of avoiding pain, ministry actually "deepens it" to "a level where it can be shared."[21] By listening to such pain, Father Bill helps them feel that their suffering is held in the memory of God.

CONGREGATIONAL CARE AFTER SUICIDE

Ralph and June do not suffer alone, but, rather, in relationship to the parish. When a suicide occurs, everyone in a community can feel dread. After an initial outpouring of support from their small group, the group began to avoid Ralph and June because they did not want to say the wrong thing. There are many reasons why parishes avoid the topic of suicide, including fear and family secrets. Parishioners who might already be depressed may consider suicide themselves (the copycat phenomenon). Others might remember a hidden family history of suicide as "an open secret" from their past that had been covered up with a euphemism: "He was just cleaning his gun."

Father Bill hopes to normalize and destigmatize suicide in its aftermath, thereby helping the parish to face rather than avoid their fears. With Ralph and June's permission, Father Bill talks about suicide openly from the pulpit and begins a three-week church school series to deconstruct common myths and preconceptions about suicide, such as the idea that suicide is an unforgivable sin. He frankly discusses how his own life was changed by Jeremy's suicide and how he wants to continue to remember Jeremy's life and avoid other occurrences of suicide. Some parishioners encourage him to stop talking about it, fearing that it will stir up painful feelings, but he knows it is better to address what is on everyone's mind. Frequently, young people need their fears addressed openly. Children also need a chance to state guilty feelings openly, including by drawing about their loss. Moving toward fears about suicide requires courage, but it can be helpful for all generations.

Often parishes need theological teaching that helps foster a faithful response to the fragmentation that comes about through suicide. The best teaching emphasizes mercy, describing suicide as a response to intolerable pain that stems from mental illness. Ministers can openly encourage their parish to affirm that God loves them. When discussing suicide from the pulpit in a homily about Saul falling on his sword, Father Bill emphasizes that the Bible never explicitly condemns suicide (see 1 Sam 31:4). He confirms that God is compassionate and merciful. In preaching on this text he emphasizes Saul's life more than his suicide, showing how a person's narrative is not confined to the way it ends.

In church school, Father Bill has a local social worker teach about suicide prevention. The social worker teaches the parish that talking about suicide does not plant the idea in anyone's head. She also mentions that if you hear someone talk about being discouraged or giving their things away, it is better to ask directly, "When I hear that kind of thing, I have noticed that sometimes people are thinking of ending their life. Has that thought occurred to you?" The social worker teaches people how to establish a "no suicide" contract with people at risk, a document in which the at-risk person agrees to call three different people before she takes her life. If a person denies they are thinking about suicide, they often feel relieved that the subject is mentioned. In all such interventions, Father Bill emphasizes that even if you miss the signs of suicide, you are not to blame if someone takes their life.

Suicide loss creates a crisis in the experiential image of God in everyone's life—the part of faith in which people cry out to God, dream, and sing. This happens at the individual level, but it also happens to the entire gathered community. Because it happens unconsciously, it can be frightening for people who are not very aware of their own feelings. June and Ralph's small group wants to pray a healing prayer for them, but they are not comfortable with this ritual. Father Bill teaches this well-meaning group that God is already present with them in their grief and that it is more important to provide long-term, supportive conversational care rather than a one-time ritual.

Ministers often feel that they should be providing guidance when comfort and accompaniment is what is required. It is important for survivors and congregations to find ways of lamenting what is lost and expressing all the ways they feel God has failed them.

By going through the process together, survivors and congregations can often find their way back to trusting in a faithful and caring God. Through compassionately coaching the parish through the trauma of suicide, Father Bill shows that it is better to face unspoken fears than to hide from them.

CONCLUSION

June and Ralph experience a pain that will not go away after Jeremy's loss. Father Bill has found a way to touch base with them during holidays and tell them that he remembers Jeremy. In this way, he has helped the family believe that they are remembered by God. In ministering to the family, Father Bill was also ministering to the broader parish for whom Jeremy's suicide created fear and doubt. He found himself coaching the parish to be unafraid of the subject of suicide by encouraging them in the knowledge that God was big enough for their fears.

Ralph has become more involved in church because of Father Bill's care, but June has dropped out entirely. Father Bill sometimes wonders if he could have done more to help her reconnect with faith, and he remembers her in his prayers. Father Bill continues to see a spiritual director after counseling the family; in his conversations with her, he talks about his continuing bonds with Jeremy. In fact, as his minister, Father Bill is a suicide survivor as well. By caring for his own story, he is faithful to the ministry of caring for the stories of others in the congregation.

FOR FURTHER REFLECTION

1. How does suicide challenge story care? What are the primary pastoral tools we should use to approach it?
2. Why does it never work to try to cheer up a suicide survivor? What might be a better pastoral aim?
3. Why does it not work to tell suicide survivors anything about God's love? In what ways does the adage *Show, don't tell* apply to the care of suicide survivors?

II

CARE
FOR
SYSTEMS

4

STORIES OF MARGINALIZED PEOPLE

Clara cleans houses for a living. She begins work at six in the morning and ends long after dark. She grew up in northern Mexico and came to the United States with her husband, who later left her. Now she raises three children by herself, and they attend the Catholic Church downtown on Christmas and Easter when she has time away from work.

Last fall, Clara hurt her back while on the job and was not able to work for several days. When she was fired for missing work, she was hesitant to ask for her job back because she was undocumented. Also because of her citizenship status, she was ineligible for unemployment insurance. When Clara goes to the church's food pantry for help, Estela, a lay minister in the parish, talks to her about her problems. Their conversation takes place in the church foyer, where she catches her breath over a cup of coffee.

"Everything has been so hard since I left Mexico," she says. "I thought the United States would give me opportunities with my family, but it's been hard."

"It's been difficult since you got here. You haven't had the opportunities you hoped for?" Estela responds.

"No, and I worry about my kids. I know that the youngest one in daycare is not treated the best when I leave him there. Well, I find bruises on his skin." Clara says. "The older ones go to a school where there's drugs and the teachers aren't paying attention. One girl got abused in the back of the classroom and the teacher was not even there."

"That sounds awful. Can you talk to the school principal?" Estela asks.

"I write her emails, but she never responds. Two or three weeks go by and she does not respond."

There is a pause in the conversation before Estela continues, "You told me about what brought you here, needing some assistance because you are laid off because of an injury. Are there any other ways we can help you while you're here?"

"I don't know," Clara says. "I feel bad when I come here. I grew up in a family that was very proud. We never depended on others for charity. Even though we were poor, we always helped others."

Estela answers, "So you feel bad reaching out for help in a time like this. I can appreciate that," she says. "But I don't think that you should blame yourself for what you are going through. There aren't a lot of opportunities when you're undocumented, and it's difficult to get enough to take care of yourself and your family."

"Thanks, that's good for me to hear. We need a doctor for the kids. If something comes up, I end up going to the emergency department after hours because the clinic in our neighborhood is only open once or twice a week."

Estela says, "I know of a neighborhood health service that's really quite good and that can help you so that you don't have to go to the ER so much."

Their conversation continues in this fashion, Estela building on Clara's comments, responding compassionately to her pain, and providing resources when appropriate. When Estela cares for Clara, she treats her as a person with dignity and vocation, a person whose worth is not defined by her immigration status, her physical health, or how much money she makes. Rather, care is communicated through a respectful relationship that reflects the image of God in Clara. In this way Estela builds a personal relationship with her, developing a needed attachment in a challenging time. When she provides resources, it is based on a relationship that is being established.

Estela helps Clara by giving her suggestions of resources that confirm her worth in a situation where no one else might be responding to her; she also helps by listening to her story and normalizing her predicament. Afterward, Estela shares the details of her conversation with Clara with the parish priest, suggesting that the church develop a program to address the needs of immigrants in her community, since much of the oppression Clara is facing is due to her undocumented status.

In what follows, we explore how to understand Clara's situation theologically using liberation theology, and we describe how to engage a cycle of social therapy to invite religious communities to respond to social needs through empowerment from social oppression. Finally, we distinguish empathy as a defining practice of pastoral care, showing how caregivers can exhibit this quality to remove roadblocks of oppression that stand in people's way.

LIBERATION THEOLOGY

The fact that Estela's conversation with Clara takes place in the church gives the meeting theological significance. Estela certainly thinks of her reasons for volunteering at the church as theological; she has been inspired by the "least of these" scenarios in the Gospels (see Matt 24). In this story, people who help others are inadvertently helping Christ even though they do not realize it is Christ that they are helping. Though Estela is a fourth-generation Mexican American, she understands what it feels like to be pushed to the sidelines, having remembered her own family's stories of immigration. Caring for Christ in the presence of a woman with undocumented status is something important to Estela's own identity.

Clara's story also shows us something distinctive about God's nature and identity, opening our eyes to the meaning of Scripture and revealing God's activity. While liberation theology has included many diverse voices, one of its important themes is that God is especially tuned to the concerns of those who are poor and marginalized. Some people are born into situations where they are more likely to face unintended violence because of their race, ethnicity, or gender. Pastoral care removes obstacles to care for someone in these circumstances, inviting us to follow God's commandment by accompanying the poor and assisting them through their struggles.[1]

The unifying theme of liberation theology is the notion that the well-being of the poor and marginalized is a special concern to God. Because it is the poor who are frequently forgotten by society and pushed to the margins, to care for them is to help them feel remembered by God. Clara is poor because she is undocumented, and she is a marginalized person because she cannot step fully into society. Liberation theology suggests that the society should not be satisfied with these conditions. Paradoxically, helping the marginalized person feel remembered by God allows the entire body of Christ to be remembered as well, since the church who forgets the poor and marginalized forgets something essential to its identity.

In his discussion of how pastoral care is rooted in the history of ancient Israel, Charles Gerkin notes that pastoral care has been incorrectly identified with the role of the sage when, in fact, it needs to reclaim its priestly and prophetic functions. In chapter 2, this framework was discussed as a way of bringing balance to pastoral ministry. Sages are responsible for practical moral guidance, whereas priests are responsible for helping the people worship. Prophets are responsible to call people back to the will and "purpose of God for the mutual care of the people, indeed for the care of all human affairs and for the earth."[2] Gerkin argues that we must reclaim the prophetic dimensions of pastoral care; by doing so we can help people remember that God demands justice for the most marginalized person.

Prophetic pastoral care invites us to transform social systems with the aim of helping people live more fully in community with one another. Clara's health care for her family and the abuse of her children are equal concerns to her own well-being. To care for her authentically, it is necessary to respond to all her systemic needs. By working to transform systems, pastoral caregivers attempt to take away unnecessary suffering such as that which comes from having inadequate access to necessary goods. As noted in the introduction, the removal of unnecessary suffering is an important goal of pastoral care.

Liberation theology is a resource for pastoral care that orients the discipline to those who are poor and marginalized in any community and invites people to accompany them to help foster their well-being. Liberation theology expresses the fact that social advocacy for the poor and marginalized best expresses God's nature. Thus God's love for those who are oppressed must be realized in some concrete ways through a transformation of the lives of the oppressed. Liberation for people, expressed in their well-being in psychological, spiritual, emotional, and physical ways, is part of the expression of the goodness of God in community. Orienting pastoral care toward such liberation requires accompanying people so they can experience more just relationships in their lives. The prophets of ancient Israel reminded people that their celebrations remained fruitless if the poor in their community were oppressed (see Amos 8:6; Isa 58). Liberation theology helps transform both individuals and religious communities to more faithfully reflect God's nature.

A CYCLE OF SOCIAL THERAPY

To provide wise pastoral care for people impacted by systems, it is important to take into account their complex social identities. Emmanuel Lartey has argued that people in communities and specific contexts have pastoral care needs that must be met, with an acknowledgment of the intersecting realities of "global issues" facing a person as well as their own "race, gender, class, sexuality, and economics."[3] Lartey offers a cycle of "social therapy" in which he takes seriously the oppression faced by persons in various aspects of their social identity in order to take pastoral action with them and on their behalf.[4] The cycle starts with a human story, then turns to social systems and policies in order to transform the conditions that led to suffering and, finally, returns to the Christian community to integrate self and system.

Estela begins the cycle of social therapy by giving Clara information about health care resources; she advocates in the community to change policies related to immigration; finally, she closes the loop by advocating that her parish address immigration reform. The following week in church, Estela introduces a prayer based on her conversation with Clara. By engaging each element of the cycle of social therapy, Estela uses Clara's narrative to invite the entire community to transform rather than ignore her story.

Clara belongs to one of 642 million transnational families, those who live across the generations in several nations, often sending remittances home but not being able to care for each other in the ways they might wish.[5] These families bear all the grief, burdens, and struggles noted in this book, but the marginalization of poverty and citizenship status makes these burdens more onerous. In her new context she has the role of taking care of children while also providing for her parents through sending remittances home. Her story underscores the fact that we live in a global world where people share multiple identities, crossing nations but frequently leaving supportive family members behind.[6]

Each of us belongs to social systems that define parts of our identities, visible and invisible. Visible identities include markers such as race, ethnicity, and gender when these are obvious from appearance.[7] Invisible identities may include realities such as national status, an invisible physical disability, mental illness, biculturality passing as white, or social class that might not be obvious.[8] Since Clara is in the United States and has dark-brown skin, she can be identified as a Latina. Yet part of her invisible identity is that she is undocumented. Because of long hours spent laboring, Clara is often an exhausted parent and cannot care for her children in the ways that she wants. Her identity as working class means that she has trouble making ends meet, and this identity can be visible or invisible. To care properly for systems, caregivers need to assess the impact of visible and invisible identities on a person's well-being.

Estela and Clara share a visible identity—they are defined as Latina by society in the United States. However, since they have been in this country for a different length of time and have different resources, Clara has more obstacles to finding well-being. The similarities between their stories can provide a point of entry for ministry to occur.[9]

By caring for Clara, Estela becomes more committed to advocating for the poor and disenfranchised in her community. One part of her work involves destigmatizing poverty; the other, alleviating it. She realizes that Clara is ashamed of her poverty and, as a result, wants to help normalize her experience. As she responds to the emotional aspects of Clara's story, she also realizes that she can take a further step in care. She can advocate to change the systems through which people like Clara are marginalized. Without attending to the need for social change, it can be easy for Estela to blame Clara for her problems or see her as an object of pity. What people describe as compassion fatigue or vicarious trauma among ministers is frequently watching social suffering and attempting to remain neutral when, in fact, what is needed is a response of shared advocacy.

Lartey's cycle of social therapy begins with a personal moment—Estela's caregiving with Clara in the moment of her crisis; it goes on to attempting to change the kinds of policy contributing to Clara's marginalization and then returns to transform religious communities.

What Estela discovers is that her community has opened a helpful food pantry ministry, but it does not engage in collective action to help prevent people needing to use the food pantry. It operates on the model of one-time charity or uplift rather than justice since many seem to believe that the poor should learn to help themselves. This lack of social awareness among her parishioners bothered Estela, for they seem unaware of the multiple obstacles to well-being that are placed in Clara's life, and how care for her must involve accompaniment that seeks to remove these barriers. Unfortunately, people do not start at the same place in American society, so that those who have less resources need more partnership to thrive.

Dominated by a white majority who has national citizenship in the United States and is affluent, the parish is one step removed from the full range of needs and concerns of the poor in their own community. It is important that the parish continue doing the church ministry of the food pantry but learn to see in new ways the people who use its services.

Seeing those entering the food pantry as struggling individuals makes it easy to muster compassion, but it also obscures the fact that most of them are being oppressed by systems as well. The parishioners might believe that the poor come from a "culture of poverty" that simply passes dysfunction from one generation to the next. Some people who serve in the pantry regularly never draw connections between their ministry and the dismantling of the social safety net in which fewer poor people can access government assistance. As an example, Estela began to see that her parish distances itself from the problems associated with Clara's family, in part because they think of themselves as being highly successful. By using the cycle of social therapy, Estela can understand visible and invisible identities in the religious community and thereby make pastoral care a more just practice.

OPPRESSION, EMPOWERMENT, AND COMMUNITY

Oppression is the abuse of power to make someone else do what you want.[10] People know when they are being oppressed because they are objectified, used only to meet another's needs and then discarded when no longer necessary. At times, individuals can oppress one another because they are being oppressed by society: this is unconscious oppression. In these instances oppression is subtler. The emotional consequences of oppression are those of seeing oneself as disposable rather than as a person created in the image of God with inalienable dignity. In Clara's case, her oppression makes her feel disposable to her husband and employer; through the lens of her faith, she learns that she is a person with dignity and a purpose.

Oppression can take place through several types of discrimination. All forms of oppression are important and need to be dealt with since they interfere with the fullness of one's vocation and, thus, need to be addressed at the same time. The multifaceted nature of oppression can be overwhelming for caregivers. It can also be honest and empowering to name all different facets.

At times people are oppressed by systems. Dominating institutions often take control over people's lives—the signs of which include "the use of violence or threats of violence, rendering the victim invisible, distortion of events, stereotyping, blaming the victim for the oppression, isolation, and emphasizing individual solutions over group support and cooperation.,.further breaking down the victim's autonomy."[11] Violence is used as a tool to break down the free will of a person that is being oppressed. Those who are marginalized sometimes face oppression and then denial from others about the fact that the oppression has occurred.

People who are oppressed may begin to doubt their own stories as they feel increasingly invisible. The beginning of oppression-sensitive pastoral care is listening to stories and believing them. Clara's employer does not have to respond to her workplace injury because of her undocumented status. The school authorities do not have to respond to the abuse that's being perpetrated against children in Clara's child's classroom because she has no social capital. In the case of immigration status, the threat of deportation is a form of power that is used to silence people and make them work harder for less.

Empathic and healing relationships directly address the injustice of oppression. Estela normalizes Clara's experience and thus indicates that she is available to establish a relationship with Clara. The invitation of relationship relates to the concept of attachment from the first chapter. Estela describes how the suffering she experiences is not that unusual among Mexican Americans she knows. She does this to help alleviate the shame that Clara perceives at having to ask for help.

Yet this step alone, of compassionate presence, can only go so far in responding to Clara's needs.

In addition to a healing relationship, Clara needs someone who will advocate for her to remove obstacles to well-being and help restore some of the conditions that could lead to flourishing. Estela informs Clara about an opportunity to receive health care at a low-income clinic in her community. All too often in clinical and chaplaincy work, ministers feel that they must only provide presence rather than getting involved in helping persons. If a listener remains at a level of responding to an individual's "feelings," it can seem naïve or disingenuous as it does not respond to the intent of the story when this intent includes a request for resources. The development of empathy and the meeting of basic needs go together in the cycle of social therapy.

To complete the cycle of social therapy it is important that Estela attempt to change her community through engagement with Clara's narrative. She makes an appointment with the priest of the parish, telling Clara's story in detail, and asks him how the church can change their ministry to meet the needs of someone like Clara, becoming more attentive to the plight of immigrants. Estela impresses on him that such a response helps the church more fully live out God's mission where the church is invited to partner with the poor.

COMMUNAL NARRATIVES

When attempting to change religious communities through a cycle of social therapy, it can help to understand and interpret the communal narratives that a given community lives by. When Estela first brings Clara's story to the parish priest, she asks him to start a program to help people without documents become naturalized citizens. In response, her priest says that her request is a political matter and not the job of the church to get involved in politics. Here, the communal narrative is that the parish is an apolitical community.

He notes that the church was started by European immigrants who faced their own sources of oppression and that now the church is focused on caring for the faithful rather than agitating for social change. He views the food pantry ministry as a nonpartisan act of mercy and insists that the church cannot go further than this. He sees this pantry ministry as extending the church's immigrant story of ethnic struggle, where the Catholic community throughout the twenty-first century sought to establish legitimacy.

The official story of the church is of third- and fourth-generation immigrants of European descent who have only recently stopped facing prejudice as they gained political power and influence. They still celebrate their Italian, Polish, and other heritages with pride, describing and honoring their hardworking ancestors. In the intervening decades, however, their ancestors have gone from being objects of discrimination to being white, indistinguishable from the white Protestants of German and Irish descent.[12]

Indeed the communal narratives of the church are built on ethnic struggle, and now the challenge is to expand that vision to others, joining ranks with them and working on their behalf. The church's food pantry had been created to craft a compassionate response to and assist the predominantly impoverished Latino community around them. While parishioners described it as a ministry of mercy that fulfilled the commission of Matthew 24, the board of the pantry was all Anglo-American, suggesting that there might be a disjunction in power and privilege between those who were the hosts of the church's ministry and the recipients who relied upon its services. The mistaken idea of host-guest is seen in the language of charity or uplift. Now the church's hopeful struggle is to build on a history of ethnic struggle, identify with the struggles, and remove the obstacles that are blocking the most marginalized people in our society from flourishing.

David Rappaport has argued that communal narratives involve a "story common among a group of people," a story that depicts the community's heroes, myths, and future.[13] In the parish where Estela serves in the food pantry, she notes that there were many Anglo-Americans who were the heroes of their parish's stories. Their pictures showed up on the walls with biographies, and gifts given by wealthy donors were described on plaques. She also saw that there were few Mexican Americans and few poor individuals who had their stories honored similarly in public ways. In fact, the only images that did show up were of Mexican Americans utilizing the soup kitchen services.

When Estela presents Clara's story, she suggests to the priest that the congregation needs to include more people like Clara to help them fully belong. One sign of a community's ability to care for marginalized people is whether it can worship with them. When Clara comes to Mass, Estela notes, she and others are relegated to the basement to meet with the Latino/a fellowship. Spanish is only spoken in this Mass and never in the English Masses held on the central floor of the church.

Estela argues that it is important for Clara to feel that she belongs on the upper level of the church, not only in the food pantry. She notes that Clara is showing strength by appearing at the food pantry to ask for what she needs, but that empowerment would only go so far unless she also sees herself represented on the church walls, in its hymns, and in its theologies. Integrated worship is thus one of the final frontiers of pastoral care.[14]

Estela also encourages the church to become more intensively involved in the advocacy for a change in policy toward immigrants. She argues that one of the most important oppressions Clara faces is her voicelessness due to her immigration status. She argues with the local priest that the church needs to contract an immigration lawyer and provide services for Clara and others like her.

The communal narrative suggests that most of the Anglo-Americans of the church still implicitly did not see Clara as one of its heroes and did not hear her story of crossing the U.S./Mexico border as one with which they could identify, even though their families had crossed similar borders in the last century. The cycle of social therapy includes meeting basic needs, advocating for social transformation, and changing the institutional culture of churches through efforts at advocacy. Yet it also requires building new communal narratives that can cross barriers of ethnic identity. This work is the basic task of pastoral imagination, which builds upon where the Spirit is already at work, expanding horizons outward.

SYMPATHY, EMPATHY, AND COMPASSIONATE ACTION

It is important to explain how transformation of pastoral imagination takes place using some familiar terms from the pastoral care literature, namely *sympathy* and *empathy*. This discussion will use these terms in radically new ways and invite readers to think about pastoral care as expanding beyond the individualistic care they are used to giving.

Sympathy is the initial building block of pastoral care, and it comes from shared experience. Sympathy relies upon *feeling with*, upon shared experience, and it is the basis of good pastoral care. Through sympathy, the caregiver says I have been there too and I understand. Estela has sympathy for Clara because she, too, has faced discrimination because she is a Latina. People often look to friendships to provide sympathy since it is often expected that friends will share similar experiences and give an "I've been there too" response.

Empathy goes beyond sympathy to explore situations with which one has no personal familiarity.[15] The crucial point of empathy is that one *does not know what the other is going through* but wants to know. In an empathic response, the caregiver does not fuse with the other's story or become overcome by it because the caregiver understands that the other is an actor in their life and that God is already present to the other. Empathy is transformative, and it is a crucial tool of pastoral care. It is difficult to listen with empathy to the tragedy of everyday life, and people need support to continue this ministry of presence. Someone operating from empathy does not share their own experience with the careseeker, but rather reflects on points of similarity and difference between their story and the careseekers, using their internal emotional response as a guidepost for engagement.

Empathy is the basic building block of pastoral care, and it ensures that the caregiver's story does not take over the counselee's agenda. Estela realizes that she cannot understand what it is like to immigrate nowadays, since her family did so during a time when it was easier. Empathy requires using a finely tuned emotional response to reflect on how one's story is different from another's and wanting to understand.

Sympathy and empathy can naturally lead to compassionate action to remove barriers to well-being.[16] This compassionate action seeks to reduce the amount of unnecessary suffering so that the same kind of sorrow will not be perpetrated again through unfair policies. Compassionate action does not take place on the other's behalf but rather in concert with the other, along with taking actions that attempt to remove the obstacles to flourishing in one's life.[17] Therapists are typically encouraged not to engage in social action for their clients with the belief that it will contaminate the agency of their clients.[18] Nevertheless, in pastoral care, there are sometimes situations where compassionate action is the only merciful response and where it would seem cruel to allow suffering to continue.

Compassionate action takes seriously the suffering that another person is going through, and it is a separate step from sympathy and empathy, which together constitute the building blocks of presence in pastoral care. These two responses alone are powerful and prophetic responses. There are times, however, when the enormity of human suffering overwhelms a caregiver, and they seek to help remove the unnecessary suffering that stems from oppression when possible. Rather than simply saying, "I'm sorry this happened to you," or "I'm trying to understand what has happened to you," this response acts in ways that attempt to prevent harm.

Theological perspectives invite religious communities to be sympathetic, empathic, and to take compassionate action as a reflection of God's identity. Liberation theology argues that God attends to the situations of those who are marginalized and that faithful people need to accompany the poor to transform the unjust systems of the world. Estela's life is radically transformed by encountering Clara's story—she begins to advocate for the rights of immigrants in her community, witnessing their stories and petitioning her lawmakers and church leaders to attend to these stories. In this case, compassionate action involves the rights and circumstances of the undocumented in their community, but it can just as easily include advocacy against the death penalty, for human rights, for just working conditions, or a variety of other concerns. Estela takes compassionate action because her own story has been so deeply impacted by Clara's that she is no longer able to tolerate watching undocumented immigrants being mistreated.

Meeting Clara's needs for health care and a safe educational setting for her children is a major step in individual pastoral care, an indispensable work of mercy that is at the heart of Christian faith. By adding compassionate action to her empathy, Estela can care for the system that made Clara's suffering more likely. This does not mean that suffering can be alleviated through social action alone, but some social action, such as the agitation during the civil rights movement in the 1960s, helped make unjust suffering less likely to occur.

This in no way minimizes the importance of emotion-centered, individual pastoral care. A ministry of pastoral presence with attention to one story is a true gift, however insignificant it may seem at the time. Nevertheless, compassionate actions at the communal level help ameliorate conditions of injustice that make pastoral care even more likely to be required later. Simply because the kingdom of God always seems out of reach does not mean that it is not somewhat closer through our participation with God in compassionate action.

CONCLUSION

Estela works with immigration rights groups in her community and is successful in helping her city become a sanctuary city. Nevertheless, she is less successful in helping her church advocate for the rights of immigrants in her community because her parish priest does not see this as a part of the community's shared narrative. This does not mean that she stops coming to church or advocating for change, but she uses what she experienced in her relationship with Clara to become involved in a network of people supporting immigrants in her community.

Estela and Clara's conversation takes place in the context of a food pantry in the church where Clara is seeking assistance. In this conversation, Estela cared for Clara's shame about accessing social services, while at the same time she provided some practical advice about local health care options that were affordable. Estela never sees Clara after this initial meeting and so she is unable to follow up on her care, but she is profoundly impacted by the encounter. Sometimes in pastoral care and counseling, careseekers drop away and there is no way of contacting them, but pastoral care with them is still meaningful. She learned that, while it was important to hear Clara's individual story of suffering, simply hearing it was not sufficient. It was also important to change the social situations in which that suffering was perpetuated so as to remove the burdens that the individual bears.

Estela experiences her relationship with Clara as a turning point in her own ministry. She feels called to live out the ancient Israelite prophetic tradition and call on her community to make more just arrangements for Clara and other immigrants who were not citizens of the United States. From her position of power, she uses her influence not only to build a bridge of empathy with Clara, but also takes compassionate action to transform the environment in which Clara lived and make unnecessary suffering less likely.

Clara is facing multiple oppressions, situations where power is being used against her and where she is being objectified—used as a means toward other people's ends. In such a situation, people frequently feel invisible and as if their voice has been ignored. By offering a pastoral response that includes the care for systems, Estela brings Clara's concerns into the public realm and helps others recognize the oppression that Clara is experiencing. In the process, there is always the possibility that Estela could try to speak *for* Clara rather than allowing her to speak for herself. However, she feels that the risk of being complicit in oppression if she remains silent is greater than the risk in overstepping some pastoral bounds.

When engaging in advocacy work, faithful people participate in God's purposes in the world. Liberation theology builds on a sense that God has already been at work in the world to create conditions of justice. When pastoral caregivers participate in advocacy, they have a chance to help offer God's promises to the world. When social therapy occurs, a community is invited to participate in the changes that God is already working in the world. One part of social therapy is empathy—a destigmatizing feeling—that renders visible experiences of suffering. The other part of social therapy is compassionate action that works to remove obstacles to flourishing.

Through her network of community activists, Estela finds a group of people that validate her identity and share many of her concerns. This group rallies around a man who had been targeted by immigration but had not committed any crime and had four small children that he needed to take care of. Through their advocacy, a stay was placed on this man's deportation order. Church leaders from other churches and immigrants' rights advocates shared common cause to help the man. Although his situation was not resolved, the network of advocacy that was created on his behalf seemed to make a difference in slowing his deportation.

In this community of advocacy, Estela finds a new group of friends who share aspects of her definition of social justice, even if they are not of her same faith. These friends mentor her in what it means to do community action, how she can write letters and call government leaders, and how she can build appropriate rest into her schedule to take care of herself. It is meaningful for her that the community of support in the immigrants' rights advocacy network seems attuned to the variety of problems immigrants face, including not having enough money, being abused by spouses, and having little access to health care or food aid. At times, this work feels overwhelming, but it is more meaningful to engage in this ministry than it is to be overcome with despair.

Estela understands that God's grace is freely offered to all and that the fellowship of the Spirit transcends her limited notions of where God could work. Although her church did not participate in the advocacy that she engaged in, she still found it to be a sanctuary and a place of spiritual sustenance. God was also bringing liberation through this community, and she continued to invite them to participate with her in the work of advocacy that she had organized in the community, encouraging them to see how God both loved them as they were and called them to become better.

FOR FURTHER REFLECTION

1. What is the difference between sympathy, empathy, and compassionate action, and under what conditions might each be necessary in pastoral care?
2. Is it necessary to share a common heritage with someone to advocate on their behalf?
3. What are some of your visible and invisible identities, and how do they impact your care and counseling?
4. What responses are required to help pastoral care reclaim its prophetic heritage?
5. What are some proper responses if your religious community does not share a social justice concern that matters to you?

5

STORIES OF ABUSE SURVIVORS

In a Lenten Ash Wednesday service, Pastor Janelle reads from the Psalm: "God is our refuge and strength, a very present help in trouble" (46:1).[1] After reading the Scripture, she prays aloud that those facing violence in their relationships may find safety, relief from harm, and relational justice.

Afterward, Pam reaches out for an appointment, realizing that her pastor might be a safe person to talk to about her problems.[2] First, Pastor Janelle assures her that she will not break her confidentiality and gives Pam some specific advice of ways that she can cover her tracks so that her husband will not know about their meeting.

Pam begins by describing how the abusive patterns in her relationship had developed. Early in their relationship her husband, Sandy, had tried to control Pam's clothing and manage her contacts with friends and family. Pam had a few friends who warned her about Sandy's controlling nature, but she loved him too much to listen to their advice. On the night of their first anniversary, he hit her and accused her of being unfaithful. He was contrite for weeks afterward. Because she thought it might have been an anomaly, Pam wanted to believe that he would never hit her again. Later, the punches, slaps, and even lockouts from their home became more common, but when Pam threatened to leave him, Sandy became suicidal and demanded that she stay with him. Their son, Kevin, was born during their fifth year of marriage. Pam hoped the abuse would stop, but it only escalated.

Listening to her story, Pastor Janelle knows that Pam is not only a person in danger, she is also a person with dignity and vocation, created in the image of God, and meant to help fulfill God's purposes. When her husband uses violence against her, he tries to undermine the unchangeable image of God that exists in her. Paradoxically, through the verbal and physical abuse, he denigrates his own personhood.

Pam's faith is an important part of her life and marriage. Even though she has depended on God as a source of strength in the past, she now feels abandoned. She used to believe quite strongly in a protective God, but now she senses that God has betrayed her. Mostly, she pictures God as being a male and describes how she must submit to God's will. She realizes that she has stopped praying as much as Sandy has become more abusive. Deep down she believes that God has forsaken her.

Pam thinks that she can only please God by being an obedient wife because of the devotional books that she has read. For as long as she can recall, she pictured the "ideal wedding," thinking often how marriage would complete her. She frequently blames herself for the problems in her marriage. Behind much of her thinking is the notion of a "divinely ordained marriage."[3] Yet the devotional literature that this concept comes from has not grappled with the ubiquity of men's violence against women in their interpersonal relationships. The crime of battering is an affront to God as well as Pam's humanity, a violation of the marriage covenant.[4] It is not Pastor Janelle's job to save the marriage or foster the reunion of the spouses.

When Pam looks for love and protection in her marriage, she finds a violence that is intent on confirming her worthlessness; the abuse translates into a sense of unworthiness before God. She wonders if God has forgotten about her because she is to blame; maybe her perceptions do not matter any longer. It is very difficult for her to believe that she is remembered by God in her suffering.

Sandy has been violent again in the last few weeks, hitting her head against the headboard and locking her out of the house. She lies to the emergency room staff about her concussion. So far, their child Kevin has not been hurt—he had been away with her parents at the time. Pam fears it might change at any moment.

Pastor Janelle is now in a complicated position. She, first, wants to explore options for safety with Pam and give her resources about the local domestic violence shelter. Since she has not encountered Sandy very often—he does not come to church—she is free to work as an advocate for Pam without interference.

SAFETY PLANNING WITH THE BATTERED

Pastor Janelle uses some active listening to make sure that Pam feels heard. She emphasizes that what has happened to Pam is not her fault. She also thinks to herself about her role as a pastor, a representative of God and interpreter of Scripture. Interpreting Pam's predicament, she concludes, *Pam is at the end of her resources and needs hope.*

Pam seeks her because she is a woman in a powerful religious position who represents God in nonpatriarchal ways. Her compassionate prayer in the season of Lent not only helps Pam feel understood; it helps her direct her suffering to God. Her faith had been one of her deepest sources of strength in the past.

Pastor Janelle understands from previous experiences with battered women that they are often unable to explore complex feelings until they leave the violent relationship, so she tries to equip her with supportive resources in her community. Pastor Janelle asks Pam what she has tried in relation to her husband Sandy. *How has she used the support of friends or family, and has she ever tried to leave?* Pastor Janelle listens carefully and does not give Pam the feeling that it is her fault or that she has done too little in response to the abuse. She tries to help Pam discover options for her life rather than be another controlling presence that tries to fix her. At the same time, she takes Pam's complex feelings seriously and listens for the nuance in her statements. Pastor Janelle understands that Pam might believe she has failed if she leaves, given how much she has invested in the relationship.

Pastor Janelle asks about their son's safety. "Are you afraid that if you stay, something might happen to your son, Kevin?" Pam confirms that she does. The pastor follows Pam's lead, noting that she thought it was a real possibility that Sandy would hurt their son. Pastor Janelle helps Pam see the options before her.

Since Pastor Janelle is a volunteer on the Domestic Violence Hotline (1-800-799-SAFE [7233]), she knows of some local shelters that have availability for women with children. Pastor Janelle describes the options in detail, underscoring their anonymity and the range of their support services. The pastor even has a "leaving kit" in her office, made up with basic toiletries and a charged cell phone that she offers to Pam.

Pam is not sure at this point if she is able to leave—there are financial reasons why this is hard—but she writes down the name and number of the shelter. Pastor Janelle goes on to describe how *coura-geous* it is for her to talk about this and reminds her about how she will guard her confidentiality. She assures Pam that she will never try to counsel her *with* Sandy since this might only give him more material to use against her.

For a highly religious person like Pam, ministerial safety planning also involves the exploration of faith. Abuse and faith have been inter-twined for Pam, so it is crucial for her faith to have more empowering sources of spirituality that will help her break from the abuse.

When Pam quotes Ephesians 5:21–22, a passage that suggests wives submit to their husbands, as evidence for why she should stay with Sandy, Pastor Janelle reminds her that it only makes sense in the context of a loving relationship where people are cared for equally and make decisions together. Pastor Janelle confirms that Pam's relation-ship with Sandy does not meet such qualifications. When Pam tells her about the sacramental nature of marriage, Pastor Janelle confirms that the violence has destroyed the marriage bond as it does in every case.[5] Pastor Janelle helps Pam see how God calls her to be an active participant in her life rather than simply passively accepting what hap-pens to her.[6] She encourages Pam to think about how God might be inviting her to something new in her life.

Pastor Janelle wonders aloud with Pam about God's presence in her life, whether she sees God as judging, in control, expecting things from her, or nurturing and empowering her. The tenor of their conversa-tion moves from these earlier controlling images of God to the later ones that are liberating. In relationship with Pastor Janelle, Pam starts to expe-rience a restoration of her faith in a transformative way.[7] Pastor Janelle quotes Scriptures that depict God as a mother bear (see Hos 13:8) and as a hen gathering her chicks under her wings (see Matt 23:37).

When she shows her a picture hanging on her office wall of God as a woman, Pam sighs deeply. In fact, Pastor Janelle states that she is starting to think about God not so much as a male ruler or father fig-ure but rather as a "female sufferer who understands."[8] Pastor Janelle understands that Pam's spirituality is diminished by the fact that *she has been asked to give up her sense of self* for a relationship,[9] and part of what restores her faith is to imagine God in ways more accurate to the richness and diversity of the scriptural tradition.[10]

Over the next two years, Pam leaves twice and comes back to Sandy each time. Pastor Janelle, not surprised by the outcome, never withdraws her ministerial support of Pam. She is oriented toward pastoral care for Pam that is more a long-term than short-term concern. Rather than trying to take control of Pam's life and plan it for her, she tells her that she respects how none of her options are easy. At times families in the church try to help Pam and sometimes get frustrated and complain that she has sought help but will not leave. Pastor Janelle emphasizes to lay leaders that it is difficult to leave abusive relationships and describes how the church can provide the kind of fiscal and emotional support that might make leaving possible.[11]

THE PASTORAL RELATIONSHIP WITH THE BATTERED

Pastor Janelle realized that, as she listened to Pam's story, she was engaged in a sacred act and that her prayerful presence helped God's love become real again to Pam. *God's presence can be made real in pastoral care by helping the abused tell their life stories.* The story itself is sacred, and a minister has a task of accompanying it as it unfolds.

It is also important that Pam reaches out to Pastor Janelle and seeks her support. Indeed, the ability to reach out for help and receive mentorship is an important spiritual skill that fosters hope. Pam's ability to access Pastor Janelle as a mentor is a sign of her dignity and vocation, an implicit trace of the Image of God.[12] The fact that Pam is able to reach out for help shows signs of her emerging ability to care for herself.

Leaving an abusive relationship often includes a spiritual transformation. Karolyn Sentner and Karen Caldwell have outlined some of the themes that emerge from religious women's stories of leaving abusers (see list below). The themes include *acknowledging the abuse* she has received and challenging perceptions of the submissive wife; *being receptive to advocating voices* that could help give her a reality check when she starts to fall into self-blame; *accepting the support of others,* including *listening for the voice of God; adjusting to new ways of living,* which include coping with financial difficulties; and *acknowledging anger and loss/fear toward God,* a set of emotions that only arises once the abuser is gone.

This journey is one that deepens self-awareness and self-esteem. It involves *awakening/looking within* by realizing that one is a person of worth, and *reconnecting with/strengthening supportive relationships.* It means *reaffirming faith-based beliefs and practices*, including discovering closeness to God. It also involves *helping others/reaching out*, since sharing the story of abuse adds to feelings of altruism, and *embracing a new perspective of self* that involves taking responsibility for the direction in her life.[13] Many of these themes appear in Pam's story.

STEPS FOR LEAVING ABUSIVE RELATIONSHIPS:

-Acknowledging the abuse

-Being receptive to advocating voices

-Accepting the support of others

-Adjusting to new ways of living

-Acknowledging anger and loss/fear

-Awakening/looking within

-Reconnecting with strengthening/supportive relationships

-Reaffirming faith-based beliefs and practices

-Helping others/reaching out

-Embracing a new perspective of self

Research indicates that in the early stage of leaving, women may feel worse before they feel better, but in the process of recovering from an abusive relationship, women often regain a sense of spirituality and faith.[14]

Pastor Janelle's care and advocacy for Pam was care for the entire family. She treated them with respect, building an alliance that bears fruit for many years. It also paved the way for Pastor Janelle's pastoral care of Pam's son, Kevin, as a young adult. Because she understands the family's backstory, she can provide wiser and more compassionate care to Kevin. Through care for the whole family, she sees Pam and Kevin as people with dignity and vocation, capable of making decisions that impact their lives. By helping Pam experience safety, Pastor Janelle also implicitly assists Sandy, Pam's abuser—who is harmed by the violence he commits as well—to experience greater wholeness. Nevertheless, Pastor Janelle's primary focus is rightly on supporting Pam through traumatic times.

While faith was a constant for Pam, her image of God had become profoundly impacted by the abuse she endured.[15] Reclaiming her faith from the betrayal of an abusive God and imagining God traveling with her, Pastor Janelle had an opportunity to help her revise her life of faith, an activity that became deeply intertwined with helping her find safety and participate in the decisions that mattered to her. The abuse Pam endured shaped her attachment to God and others, and deeply impacted her sense of self. Yet Pam is not alone; and although her situation is shared by many, understanding the systemic context of battering helps clarify what is needed in response.

WHO IS BATTERED AND WHAT ARE THE SIGNS?

Battering is a systemic problem that is widespread in the United States. Leaders of the Seattle Center for Prevention of Sexual and Domestic Violence maintain that the average minister will see about fourteen cases of domestic violence annually and should be attuned to survivors' experiences.[16] Ministers ought to be sensitive to the social cues of violence in relationships, such as monitoring behavior, criticism, and cutting off relational resources. It is important to stand with a survivor and believe them, since male ministers often tend to side with the male abuser.[17]

According to the National Coalition of Domestic Violence, one quarter to one half of all women in the United States experience severe physical abuse in their relationship at some point in their lifetime.[18] Battering is a problem that reflects outdated cultural norms that identify women as "belonging" to men. According to Pamela Cooper-White, "Battering is abusive behavior that *intimidates and controls the battered partner, with the purpose of establishing and maintaining authority.*"[19] Battering is a crime and it should be prosecuted rather than handled in the privacy of the home or family.

Battering includes behaviors such as gaslighting—trying to persuade someone that their perceptions are not true—and limiting their access to finances. The threats, intimidation, and denigration of battered partners is a form of oppression that seeks to put women "in their place" because of insecurity on the part of male perpetrators. Because of its prevalence and severity, intimate partner violence against women deserves sustained attention and is the primary focus of this chapter, primarily because of its prevalence and devastating impact on women's lives.[20] Although men are sometimes battered in a relationship, they have more options to leave the relationship and tend not to be in as great a danger.

Judith Bula Wise describes oppression as any situation where power and dominance are used over another person, and intimate partner violence meets the categories of oppression. One of the effects of oppression is to make the person into an object to serve another's needs. Prevalent intimate partner violence is one of the most important forms of oppression because it invites an entire gender to "silence the self."[21]

There is no one profile of a battered woman. Battering happens across social class and ethnic identities. Battering always occurs in a context, and the social and cultural identity of the battered partner is significant in determining the decision to leave. For example, recent immigrants from Mexico, South Asia, and other locations face barriers of language, culture, and racism as they seek to leave violent relationships, especially if they are undocumented. According to Shamita Das Dasgupta, courts in the United States have even suggested that domestic violence cannot be prosecuted in some groups because it is part of the culture.[22]

There are further obstacles to helping immigrant women leave battering spouses. Often, immigrant women seeking help in domestic violence shelters find no one who speak their first language; these women frequently lack resources to leave abusive relationships. Immigration policy fosters the harmful traditional notion that wives belong to their husbands by allowing women to obtain citizenship through the husband. Caring for battered immigrant women requires helping them find language-specific resources and build the necessary financial base for independence.

The face of battering in the United States is as diverse as the culture. Battering happens in gay and lesbian relationships as well as heterosexual ones. Gays and lesbians lack access to shelter services and can be arrested by police if they call for help. Blacks in the gay and lesbian community are more likely to face homicides in their partnerships, while younger LGBTQ victims experience more sexual violence. Additionally, transgender people are more likely to experience abuse than others in the LGBTQ community. According to the most recent data, poverty worsens the effects of intimate partner violence in the LGBTQ community.[23] Economic factors, such as widespread unemployment, can also lead to higher rates of battering.[24]

Nevertheless, it is worth emphasizing that battering can happen to anyone, even people with many cultural and social resources, and in these circumstances, ministers need to be in a role of equipping battering victims to experience safety. Pastor Janelle followed the "woman-defined advocacy" approach laid out in Davies et al.'s *Safety Planning with Battered Women.*[25] It is an approach that works with women to assess their current situation and help them take the next steps that they discern as important for their growth. The method is different from telling women what to do. "As battered women analyze the risks they and their children face, some will conclude that physical violence is not their greatest risk, whereas others will conclude that leaving increases their risks."[26] The approach is similar to what Christie Cozad Neuger describes as "helping women make choices."[27] Although there are many risks involved with staying, women need to be empowered and given the tools to make important decisions in their lives.

It takes an average of 11.7 years for women to leave an abusive situation, and ministers need to be attentive to that fact and able to do long-term planning with women seeking to leave a relationship.[28] It also means that parishes that seek to help battered women need to be oriented toward long-term accompaniment rather than a *quick fix* or *rescue* model. Care for those leaving intimate partner violence is long-term pastoral work. It is difficult for people who have not worked with battered spouses to understand how deeply the messages of worthlessness can be internalized, and not get frustrated when it is hard for women to leave.[29]

SOME PRACTICAL ADVICE

Since battering is so pervasive and ministers feel less prepared than they should be to handle it, in this section some practical advice will be given as to how to protect families facing battering.

DON'T...

tell a battered person what to do.

tell a battered spouse to pray more or that she can save the relationship.

pretend that battering "does not happen here" by never mentioning it in religious communities.

shame the battering survivor.

counsel the batterer and the battered together.

shame a battered person for not leaving.

accept the batterer's excuses of having a short temper or an alcohol problem.

testify on the batterer's behalf or write statements to the court on behalf of the batterer.

expose the address of a private domestic violence shelter to a batterer.

DO...

confirm that you believe the reports of abuse, stating that the person is not at fault for being abused.

state that abuse is a crime.

assess the safety of children and report abuse to Child Protective Services, a phone number that should be available in your local area. If your local system is underfunded, work to raise public awareness of the problem and advocate for better wages for staff.

include cards in the bathroom at your religious community stating, "Are you being abused in your relationship?" Include the phone number of the National Domestic Violence Hotline: (1-800-799-SAFE [7233]).

attend a seminar on domestic violence.

have "leaving packets" at the ready with basic toiletries and a charged cell phone for women who want to leave.

tell stories about battered partners at the pulpit and in Christian education contexts.

ask those who are battered about what their options are and help them expand the range of their choices.

support your local domestic violence shelter and volunteer on the hotline to help others who are battered leave abusive situations.

talk about battering as something that happens in the church and offer concrete steps for the safety of those in battering relationships.

The counseling of battering victims may test the minister's resolve and make the minister grapple with questions that she has never addressed. It can be challenging on a psychological and even physical level. Those caring for these difficult stories need someone else who can care for their own narratives. Grappling with the extent of harm caused by perpetrators can be particularly challenging to the faith of new ministers, and continuing education from the domestic violence community with support to address the issue wisely can help ministers steward their own painful emotions when it comes to battering.

RECONCILIATION AND FORGIVENESS

In the process of counseling abused spouses, some ministers raise the issue of forgiveness rather than helping the battered spouse seek safety. Such an approach may give the spouse the idea that she is theologically mandated to return to or save the marriage. While assuming implicitly that the best course of action is acceptance, forgetting, and excusing the behavior, they mistake true forgiveness and reconciliation.[30] While forgiveness is indeed a part of the Christian faith, it is a red herring early in the process of recovery from spousal abuse. The minister needs to be attuned rather to the safety of the battered spouse as the primary priority. Nevertheless, since forgiveness is so frequently misunderstood in this setting, the difference between forgiveness and reconciliation will be explored further, along with some appropriate practices regarding the notion of forgiveness in counseling.

Forgiveness requires understanding interpersonal harm and grappling with it, apart from a discussion of the restoration of relationship. If an abused partner blames herself, she is not ready to forgive because she has not grappled with the harm that has been done and is wishing simply to brush the problem under the carpet.

Forgiveness and reconciliation are God's activities in the world. Christians believe in the presence of sin and the fact that all need God's redemption. Likewise, Christians believe that God's salvation has the promise of redeeming sin and correcting what is deeply flawed.

Christians faithfully pray the Lord's Prayer and sometimes feel as though they should be responsible to forgive one another. Theologically, while it makes sense, domestic violence shatters simplistic understandings of forgiveness.

On the vertical dimension, God has forgiven all humanity and his grace allows life to flourish. Yet it is not possible by extension for Christians to expect battered spouses on the horizontal to instantly be able to forgive their batterers. To expect them to do so is to distort the good news of the Christian faith. The fact that God is at work reconciling Godself to the world in Jesus Christ does not imply that any couple experiencing violence needs to be reconciled to one another; safety and justice are the only conditions under which reconciliation can occur.

In the initial stages of recovering from a battering relationship, all questions of forgiveness and reconciliation tend to obscure harm and damage, and cover over injustice. Al Miles states, "Forgiveness is an especially complicated issue for survivors of domestic violence, particularly if they've been raised in a religious faith, such as Christianity."[31] Simply forgiving benefits the perpetrator. Thus the minister's primary aim should be to create the conditions in which safety can emerge for the battered spouse, as Pastor Janelle did in Pam's case.

Reconciliation differs from forgiveness since it implies the restoration of a relationship. A common mistake is to think of forgiveness as implying reconciliation; it does not. For reconciliation to occur with an abuser, the abusive behavior must stop, the abuser needs to be in treatment for several years without any relapses, and the battered partner must achieve financial and emotional independence from the relationship.

Reconciliation requires several key conditions. The most important is that an unequal power relationship becomes one of shared power. Reconciliation should never be *pushed* by a pastor who wants an abusive relationship to be restored for the sake of the marriage. Violence in a relationship destroys the marriage bond and creates conditions in which divorce is possible, a fact that has been agreed upon by leading figures of many denominations, including the United States' Catholic bishops.[32] Authentic reconciliation is the fruit of a lengthy process in which safety is established and unequal power relationships are redistributed.

Forgiveness is an individual process in relationship between the victim and God in which a person releases the claim the harm has on her life. Only through a prolonged process of coming to grips with the harm that has been done can a person forgive their abuser. Someone who denies that abuse happens or blocks out the physical and emotional consciousness of the abuse cannot be said to have forgiven the abuser.

As many survivors have concluded, forgiveness is *for the survivor* and not for the abuser.[33] It may or may not come with cognitive empathy, an ability to imagine what was going on in the mind of the abuser. Forgiveness is unilateral. It can occur where there is no restoration of relationship through a process of internal reflection and spiritual exploration. It cannot be encouraged by any outside party and should not be offered as an end to the spiritual journey. By establishing forgiveness as the end of a developmental process, ministers and counselors mistake it for the mystery it is, thinking that they can work ahead or plan for it.

Forgiveness is part of the mystery of the spiritual life. It is a unilateral process that occurs for the sake of the domestic violence victim and on their behalf. Thus it should never be raised as a topic while intervening in situations of battering. In other words, *the pastoral imperative is not even to mention the notion of forgiveness with the battered partner*, but rather to do everything possible to help the battered spouse become free from the harmful conditions of her life, establish her own self-worth apart from the partner, and no longer blame herself for what has happened. If forgiveness is raised *by the battered person* at a late stage in the process of establishing safety and independence, ministers should carefully distinguish it from reconciliation. Forgiveness can be discovered as an important stage of healing, only when Sentner and Caldwell's later themes (listed earlier) of grief processing, reconnecting with oneself, and establishing independence from the partner have been achieved. Below is a schema which lay out the key conditions and differences between reconciliation and forgiveness.

RECONCILIATION

-A peer-to-peer relationship

-Equal decision-making power

-Batterer aware of their own monitoring

-Not using children as a pawn

-Equal dignity and a sense of respect

-Absolute lack of coercion

FORGIVENESS

-Aware of trauma's impact

-Not self-sacrificing

-Chosen without coercion by a religious group

-For the battered spouse and not the batterer

-Is unilateral and for the sake of the battered

-Does not imply the restoration of relationship

The misplaced emphasis on forgiveness in Christian counsel, as well as the confusion between forgiveness and reconciliation, obscures the content of this important notion for faithful people struggling with battering. The best pastoral practice in pastoral ministry is to avoid the subject of forgiveness but help the person seek safety.

CONCLUSION

Sentner and Caldwell mention that many women go on to care for themselves and advocate for others as a part of separating from abuse. Pam, for example, goes back to community college at night and finishes an associate degree. Pastor Janelle is there at the graduation; Sandy is away on a trip. Pastor Janelle gives Pam a plaque with her favorite verse about God being like a mother bear. This image was one of strength and fortitude for Pam, and she gets tears in her eyes as she reads it.

Keeping faith with the memories of suffering means listening to them and keeping the person in mind. The experience of battered spouses requires something more: woman-defined advocacy, which itself helps people feel remembered by God. Engaging in the practice of advocacy may lead directly to personal growth for battered spouses. Perhaps Pastor Janelle's advocacy for Pam ended up being helpful for her son in his identity development as well.

As with so many stories in pastoral care, Pam's narrative seems unfinished because she remains in a relationship in which violence has occurred. Yet, through Pastor Janelle's "woman-defined advocacy" and theological reflection, she has gained more tools to resist the abuse. By keeping faith with her memories, Pastor Janelle has literally helped Pam restore her faith by coming to realize that God cares for Pam's dignity and vocation, seeing her as a person of worth.[34]

Pastor Janelle has realized that, through listening to a battered spouse, she is listening to God. Her attention to her story helped Pam feel remembered by God and helped her attach to Pastor Janelle and others outside her marriage. When Pastor Janelle prays the Psalms, she frequently thinks of Pam and her family, and she cries out to God for justice for them. At the same time, she believes that as she hears Pam's story, she directs it to God in the form of lament, a God that listens when we care for other's stories.

FOR FURTHER REFLECTION

1. Intimate partner violence is one of the most frequently cited reasons for visiting with clergy, but survivors often feel like ministers fall short in this critical area. Why do you think this is the case?
2. Many denominational sources agree that violence in a relationship destroys the marriage covenant/sacrament, and that ministers should not urge battered spouses to stay in the relationship. Given what you have learned in this case study, what are the implications of this for pastoral practice?
3. Many battered spouses stay in a relationship to try to change the abuser. How could you convey that this is God's job and help the battered partner find safety for themselves and their families?
4. What is wrong with asking battered spouses to forgive their partners?

6

STORIES OF
ADDICTS AND THEIR FAMILIES

Samantha is finally picked up by the police because she has stolen from her divorced father, James, yet she feels a sense of relief, saying to herself, "I'm tired of running." She has been using prescription drugs and alcohol since she was thirteen, but her problem has intensified. She has tried to avoid James and ignored his offers of help. In the last several years, she has begun selling her own and stolen possessions for drug money. Attempting to avoid arrest, her addiction takes over her life. Yet she is not alone. Since there are few social and job opportunities in her region, prescription pill abuse is on the rise.

James has tried everything to help Samantha stop. "What did I do wrong?" he asks himself. "What is going to happen next?" As he rearranges his life to cope with his daughter's addiction, James has stopped attending church and has withdrawn from family members. He constantly thinks back on memories from her childhood to discover the source of her problems. "What did her mother do wrong?" James wonders, since she left the relationship years ago and now is only intermittently in touch with Samantha. "I can't believe you helped her find drugs!" James tells Samantha's brother Joe, who is no longer using and shares his father's concern about his sister's drug use. Finally, when Samantha steals from her father, he decides to call the police. At the court-ordered treatment center, Samantha meets Father Roger, a licensed addiction counselor who can accompany this family in early recovery.

Addiction is a complex issue and can only be addressed through a systems approach that considers heredity, social context, and family relationships. The pastoral care of adolescents who use substances is of specific concern. While adolescents may not meet clinical criteria for substance abuse disorder, early and frequent use can change their brain patterns, making a diagnosis more likely in later life.[1] Because of the prevalence of the problem, many parents in churches, hospitals, and parishes struggle with their adolescents' drug or alcohol use.[2] Pastoral care can help bring the topic out of the shadows, allowing it to be a safe subject for discussion.

At the same time, by starting the road to recovery while still young, adolescents can establish crucial skills and spiritual dispositions to enhance well-being. Early recovery is a process of separating from a destructive pattern to build new life experiences apart from the substance abuse.[3]

Addiction is a disease, rather than a moral failing, in which will-power has been overtaken by substances that initially create rewards in the mind. A consequence of addiction is a disrupted spirituality for the addict and her family. Because addiction is also a response to spiritual needs, replacing the craving with faith practices can lead to a more profound recovery.

Father Roger, a parish priest and addictions counselor, helps Samantha and James in the process of recovery. He helps Samantha replace addiction with spiritual practice rather than simply stop using. As in all recovery, Samantha needs to learn to trust another to recover. Because of his wisdom and kindness, and because of her openness to help, Father Roger can establish a relationship of trust with her. Through this caregiving bond she can begin to trade the symptom for the relationship. In the process, she can begin replacing drugs with an exercise routine and a spiritual practice of contemplative prayer. He also assists her father James in learning to trust God again despite how he feels betrayed by Samantha in her addiction. Wise addiction treatment includes spiritual practices, family systems interventions, and advocacy in the social sphere that leads to treatment, not criminalization.

SAMANTHA'S HABIT

Samantha started using drugs at thirteen, and this became a daily habit by age seventeen. At first, she used at concerts and outings with friends. Later, she began to use by herself, getting high before school. She developed a special language for her drugs and habitual ways of storing them. Finally, she sold drugs to her friends so she could use at higher rates.

As Samantha used, she became part of an outsider and marginalized culture.[4] While she had grown up in a traditional church environment and spent time in a sheltered neighborhood, through drug use, she started acting the role of the rebel. She quit going to church and entered a group of drug-using friends. Now she defines herself as spiritual but not religious, feeling uncomfortable in a traditional environment. These changes are more a result of the way society treats drug users than the dynamics of drugs themselves: if drug users were less criminalized, they might not be so profoundly marginalized.

James first found Samantha's pain pills in her purse when she was fifteen and denied the severity of her problem. Eventually, as he became completely focused on it, his way of life started to revolve around her addiction, James always asked Samantha what she was doing every weekend. Because of these conversations, Samantha started to *feel like* the problem. He sent her away to special military-style addiction treatment summer camp when she was sixteen, but she returned bitter.

James desperately wanted Samantha to stop, and Samantha wanted, just as desperately, to define her own life apart from what she saw as her father's oppressive intrusion. Over time, Samantha and James experienced diminishment in their physical health and spiritual lives. Addiction eroded trust as their emotional dynamic became increasingly oppositional.

James faced double alienation: a single father with custody of his child and the pressure to create the perfect family to maintain custody. As Samantha's use escalated, he believed it was a verdict on his parenting.

At crisis point, punctuated by uncomfortable silences and untold truths, Samantha's seventeenth year became a turning point in their relationship. Just when she should have been preparing to leave home to make her own way as a young adult, she was on the brink of, in James's words, "throwing her life away." When Samantha stole from him to support her habit, he called the police.

When the police arrived and searched James and Samantha's small apartment, looking for evidence, James was embarrassed by their visit and frightened that it was because of him that his daughter encountered the criminal justice system. Paradoxically, he was also relieved that Samantha might finally be getting the help she so desperately needed. Because of the dearth of treatment options in their area, being held by the police may be the beginning of serious recovery.

EARLY RECOVERY

REESTABLISHING TRUST

Thankfully, with a recent arrest, Samantha enters a twelve-step program and receives counseling with a certified addiction counselor, Father Roger. She seems able to establish a therapeutic relationship with him and for this reason seems to be headed on the right track. After a brief inpatient detoxification treatment, Samantha returns to her father, who accepts her back into his home reluctantly because he has few other options.

James expects Samantha to be able to recover with just one series of outpatient treatments. James asks Father Roger about what he can do to save Samantha, and he emphasizes that recovery from addiction is a *process* and not a magic bullet. By kindly accompanying them and helping to address their preconceptions, Roger assists Samantha and James in their difficult journey. In addition, he becomes an important person in Samantha's and James's recovery because he imparts to them the lesson that they are deeply loved, understood, and accepted by God. This becomes the basis for later recovery.

Samantha feels divided. On the one hand, she wants to stop treatment, and on the other hand, she is curious about what Roger has to offer. Attracted to what she saw as the liveliness in Roger's personality, she realizes that something is missing in her own life in addiction. She thinks, on some inarticulate level, that if she could learn some of the lessons Roger had learned in his life, she might be able to recover.

DEVELOPING HOPE

Addicts can benefit from a generous and kind exploration that helps them learn what recovery might look like for them. Father Roger uses motivational interviewing, a technique that helps an addict discover their own interest in recovery and thus begin to hope. Instead of dwelling on the symptoms of addiction and their manifestations, the approach Father Roger employs does not rely on shaming or scolding, and it does not necessitate making a person realize that they have "hit bottom." Instead, he asks open-ended questions about her individual goals and how her life might be different if she were not abusing drugs.

In motivational interviewing, a caregiver explores a person's ideals and hopes for themselves in detail, shedding light on addiction as something that is keeping the person from reaching their goals. Motivational interviewing helps the addict explore hopeful narratives that help establish early recovery.[5]

Father Roger asks respectful questions, such as "Why did you stop your last relapse?" and lingers on Samantha's answers, helping her build a story about what she treasures and values. The idea behind his questions is that Samantha should return to whatever she cared about that made her stop, and explore the meaning of this goal or value, deepening and enriching this description so that it can accompany her into the next stage of her life. Such questions can be asked even if a person begins treatment through the criminal justice system. Early addiction recovery helps people get in touch with what matters most, an implicitly spiritual act, since it touches on dignity and vocation, reinforcing that she is both created in the image of God and worthy of a life of purpose.

It takes a while for Samantha to feel ready to enter recovery. Motivational interviewing helps Father Roger bridge the lack of readiness and discover an emerging interest in recovery.[6] Change occurs very slowly in addiction recovery, and it requires changes in behavior as well as developing a belief that recovery is possible.[7]

STAGES IN EARLY RECOVERY

Pre-contemplation: does not recognize the need for change or believe that it is impossible

This is where Samantha is when she goes into police custody.

Contemplation: awakens to the need for change but is not yet ready for change

As Samantha begins motivational interviewing, she realizes she values life apart from addiction.

Preparation: has a growing sense of self-efficacy as we develop a plan of action

As Samantha builds life skills such as shopping and managing her finances, she feels more confident in recovery.

Action: takes the necessary steps to change

Samantha can formulate treatment goals for herself.

Maintenance: does what is needed to make change permanent

Through the practice of centering prayer and exercise, Samantha engages these steps.

Termination: integrates change behavior so that the risk of returning to former behaviors is small

Samantha is not quite at this stage, yet it is foreseeable that she might be in the future.

Before the arrest, Samantha was at the *pre-contemplation* stage. Because of Father Roger's intervention and the action of the Holy Spirit, she moves into the *contemplation* stage during outpatient treatment. By the end of this chapter, Samantha will be at the *action* stage of recovery, but it does not mean she will stay there. Many addicts go through stages in which they are not ready to change, think of changing, are undecided, are somewhat ready to change, and very ready to change all in the same day! Family care for addicts can be frustrating because family members expect quick movement through these changes. Families need to learn to care for their own anxiety as the addict slowly changes.[8]

The suggestion that addicts do *not* need to get to the worst possible state to take personal responsibility, for example, "hit bottom," is one of the most important new realizations from addiction research. Instead of a once-and-for-all model of hitting bottom, addiction can frequently build skills for recovery through prevention, education, and resourcing even before facing serious life consequences.[9] Many in society can achieve recovery earlier than in previous generations because they have access to more tools and resources. Most importantly, people can recover through the intervention of many caregivers in concert with the action of the Holy Spirit.

BUILDING LIFE SKILLS

As she develops an interest in recovery, Samantha needs to develop life skills that can help her cultivate her painful emotions. Since the addiction dulled painful emotions that were also a sign of things that were wrong in her life, through recovery she must face these parts of her life with compassion. Father Roger teaches journaling to help her process thoughts and remain present with painful feelings rather than running away from them.[10]

When she feels nostalgia about the party scene with her old friends, she writes about her thoughts in the journal, describing in detail what led up to them. "Stinking thinking," when an addict ruminates on how life was better during the addiction, is one of the chief factors that leads to relapse.[11] Father Roger helps her interrupt this thinking by imagining possible consequences that could ensue if the party life she recalls was taken to its logical conclusion.

Journaling can help persons with addiction identify triggers that cause heart palpitations and salivation, which physiologically prepare the body to use again. Simply being hungry, angry, lonely, or tired, known as HALT by trained counselors, can lead a person to be triggered to return to the addiction. All too often people are not even consciously aware of what leads them to relapse; journaling followed by talking about the journal entries helps build a space for meditative reflection on one's embodied feelings.

Sometimes triggers come from negative thoughts such as the judgment "I am a failure because I haven't gotten a job." Such thoughts can be linked unconsciously to feelings of shame, anger, or sadness—deep feelings that a person with addiction frequently thinks but cannot express. At other times, triggers are beliefs and expectations: "I am better than that other person, so why did she get all the credit?" and "I am a bad person because I stole from people," or "I must be a loser because I cannot get a job." Journaling is a beneficial exercise that builds bridges between unconscious thoughts, feelings, and actions.

Sometimes triggers are behavioral, such as going past the same bar where one used to drink or receiving a social media message from a former friend with which one used drugs. For example, Father Roger helped Samantha slow down and explore her primary triggers, expressing her own judgments and beliefs about herself in the process. In trying these triggers out, she was able to intervene in them before she returned to the addiction.

SPIRITUAL APPROACHES TO ADDICTION TREATMENT

Addiction and disease disrupt spirituality, knocking the inner compass off kilter. An indispensable part of treatment is replacing addictive behavior with spiritual practice to reorient the sense and lead to self-forgiveness. Unless the core theological questions of selfhood are addressed, simply repressing addiction has been shown ineffective. Instead, addiction must be replaced by spirituality.

As a spiritual condition, addiction includes bonding with a substance to fill an inner void. According to Augustine, "Our hearts are restless until they rest in thee."[12] Addiction is an image, however dim, of how desire for God can be wrongly formed into desire for substances. The spiritual component of desire morphs quite quickly into something else as the bond to the substance becomes more important than all other relationships. Through the dynamics of habit, what begins as a mere behavior gets hardened into a disposition.[13] In the end, addiction is demonic, with people sacrificing their relationships and their interests for the sake of something that is ultimately unsatisfying. There is no shred of pleasure left.[14]

Psychological theory can be helpful in explaining addiction but lacks theological depth because of its pragmatism. In her book *The Wounding and Healing of Desire*, Wendy Farley identifies the many ways that the human personality seals itself off from God, calling their forms of self-defense the *passions*.

Through elaborate strategies of denial and self-sufficiency, the soul attempts to stand on its own, avoiding the God who seeks union with it. The *passions* are the names for strategies of God avoidance. Passions include rage and addiction, and the feelings of fear and terror. Seemingly good attributes, such as perfectionism or a need to get everything right, can likewise be expressions of the passions, being used to protect a person from feeling vulnerable and thereby separating the self from God. Passions are the names for human inability to trust God as worked out in practice.

Dorotheus of Gaza described hell as the undiluted presence of one's passions.[15] Although they are meant to protect people, the self-defensive measures of the passions are painful to the soul, numbing it from the union that God wished to complete with the soul. In recovery, one's consciousness of former alienation from God can become almost unbearable and the sensation of loss comes flooding back.

The idea of the *passions* normalizes coping mechanisms that keep people far from God. Farley argues that many of us are just as divided from God's love as "a most degraded drug addict is," since even though we do not turn to drugs to soften the blows of daily life, it is possible that we turn to work, to family, or the quest of perfection for the right answers.[16] Thus nonaddicted people can be empathic to the addicted once they come to realize the defense mechanisms that they use to protect themselves from vulnerability to God.

Recovery from addiction is thus a spiritual journey in which persons reconnect their moral compasses and their hopes for themselves, becoming "more fully alive" in the process.[17] Because it involves allowing feelings that have been long denied into consciousness, the process can be excruciating.

Thus addiction recovery is often a parable of God's grace; as in twelve-step and other treatment programs, people slowly discover the will of God in their lives. It also helps family members work with their own spiritual dispositions as family members struggle with addiction. Recognition of this grace culminates in self-forgiveness, the fruit of insight and spiritual growth, relying upon the notion that one is forgiven by God and can participate with God in a meaningful existence.

Since addiction points to the transcendence of human beings, it does not work to simply repress it, but it must be replaced with practices of faith. Recovery practices such as contemplation and meditation, as well as acts of service or mercy, help a person with addiction connect to the inner and outer world.

Father Roger was able to help Samantha slow down the spiral of shame-based thoughts and ask her if she could do some spiritual practices when these thoughts are worst, typically in the morning. She begins to pray with rosary beads, moving her fingers gently over them, in a practice she had been taught by her maternal grandmother. Because she once shared this practice with her mother, it is also an important link to her mother's legacy. By fulfilling spiritual, practical, and lineage functions, her spiritual practice helps address family systems as well as personal psychological needs.

TWELVE STEPS OF ALCOHOLICS ANONYMOUS

By far the most common spiritual approach to addiction treatment is the Twelve Steps of Alcoholics Anonymous,[18] but we have delayed discussing them until now because they are not the only way to recover from addiction. Nevertheless, the Twelve Steps remain the most important spiritual program for addiction. They use the term "higher power" instead of being linked to any specific faith tradition. Still, the rich practices of joy and surrender at the heart of Christian faith are expressed in twelve-step philosophy. Based on the Oxford Group's model of recovery and the spiritual breakthroughs of Bill Wilson, it relies on a pattern of storytelling and mentorship that meets the emotional needs of members and works equally well for people with addiction and their families.[19]

In Samantha's case, it was helpful once she chose the right group. She started in a Narcotics Anonymous group for women only. In group, she found several women who she began to trust, thus indicating that she was open to a mentoring relationship.

Twelve-step groups are free and available in many communities; the only requirement for membership is an interest in recovering. Through her fellowship in a twelve-step group, she realized that she was powerless over addiction, took an inventory of her personality issues, and started to make amends to those she had harmed.[20] Note: The twelve steps focus not so much on the causes for Samantha's addiction but rather her responsibility to "clean her own side of the street."

Samantha achieved three months sober in Narcotics Anonymous before she reached the fourth step, an event in which the addict confesses their moral failures to someone who is trusted. Samantha chose Father Roger for this since he had some acquaintance with the steps. When she shared her fourth step, she told her secrets. She had once crashed into a parked car when high and ran away, too embarrassed and afraid to take responsibility. She also talked about how her life in the disease of addiction had come to be structured around established patterns such as envy, jealousy, or grandiosity, that the twelve-step program calls "defects of character."[21]

Through the twelve-step program, Samantha learned that personality habits and traits have developed around years of active addiction. Underneath, she realized that she had built her life on suspicion, believing that others could not be trusted because she did not feel worthy of their love. While she is not culpable for the disease of addiction, to recover she must come to grips with the personality traits that she used to sustain her addictive behavior as a part of her recovery.

Since only about a third of people are sober after their first year in AA, it is important to offer more treatment options than twelve-step groups alone.[22] Because it is free and widely available, it is a frequently used resource by pastoral ministers, but even if people cannot use the steps, they can recover through other forms of therapy and spiritual practice.

A combination of twelve-step treatment, counseling psychotherapy, and spiritual practice means that Samantha was moving into the action stage of recovery.[23] She was beginning to make her own goals related to her treatment and learning how to self soothe when she felt shame. This enabled her to reach out to others who needed help. Defining her own goals in therapy, rather than doing so under the pressure to change, meant that she was making considerable progress.

FAMILY RELATIONSHIPS IN EARLY RECOVERY

Through the process, Samantha continues living with her father, James. However, just because she starts to get sober, all their relationship problems do not disappear. He always wants to know what she is doing, and he feels scared if she seems upset. He also eagerly waits to see what will happen to Samantha; he has elevated expectations for her recovery and low self-focus, a recipe that often leads to conflict.

She finds that, as she recovers, she feels increasingly irritable, sometimes taking these feelings out on her dad. One of the things she expects from him is for him to forgive her instantly for what she has done. As Beverly Conyers notes, "When addicts begin to recover, trust is one of the first things they long for, but it may be one of the last things they are able to establish in their lives."[24] In early recovery, more stories come out about what Samantha had done in active addiction. Thus trust erodes between her and James at the very moment Samantha feels like she should have earned it back.

Living with her father becomes too intense, so after two more months, Samantha moves into an apartment building in a nearby neighborhood, believing that her sobriety might not survive if she stays with her father. Incidentally, at this point, her father begins attending Alcoholic Anonymous meetings for himself, reconnecting with a rich spiritual source of purpose that had been diminished through his focus on his daughter.

When Samantha is at five months into recovery and everyone thinks she is doing better, she feels like she is in hell. Addiction, one of her primary defense mechanisms, had nearly dulled her sense of spirit, along with the capacity to grieve what she was losing in addiction. Now that she has stopped, she feels everything catching up with her and mourns the time she had lost in addiction. She has given up the friendships that had been based on drug use but has yet to replace them with more healthy connections.

Running, swimming, and biking to gain control of her racing thoughts, she discovers that daily exercise is an important part of caring for her body. She takes a program at a vocational center to help her develop some skills that she can use in the workplace. When she begins to feel afraid and her thoughts start to race, the new routines help her avoid the existential panic and feel her desire to connect to God again. Addiction attempts to avoid pain and, in the process, blocks out God. Thus her ability to feel pain is a hopeful sign since it is associated with spiritual awakening.[25]

Healing from addiction often leads to reconciliation with estranged family and friends. Father Roger asked her to reconnect with her estranged mother. This is difficult for her to imagine, but he clarified that he is not saying that she needed to forgive her mother for everything she had done to her or to care for her mother. Rather, the goal is simply to reach out and try to understand her mother, through which she might gain insight into her own life and personality. She will need to have sobriety maintenance programs in place so that she does not slip because of the potential emotional turbulence.

MAINTENANCE AND SLIPS

Simply becoming sober does not solve all of Samantha's problems. She is still behind educationally and has a misdemeanor police record. At twenty-eight, she has spent more time in her life addicted than she has sober. This means that recovery will necessarily be a prolonged process. She finds it hard to answer the question "Who will I be without addiction?"

Maintenance in recovery means that more of life is absorbed by recovery-based activities than addictive ones. This definition challenges the dichotomous definition of addiction recovery as sobriety. Twelve-step programs emphasize sobriety but do not make it a precondition for coming to meetings, acknowledging the back and forth movement of recovery. Recovery is not a stable state, but a constant negotiation.

Samantha has been feeling particularly low when her friend Jason comes into town for a visit. She meets him at a local bar, gets drunk, and then uses prescription pills. She has been sober for eighteen months at this point and has a decision to make. She can either stop and talk to her support system or enter a full relapse. Choosing the former, she sets up an emergency appointment with Father Roger that helps her stabilize. She also returns to the twelve-step group she had stopped attending.

She realizes that she needs to be surrounded by the reality of addiction and its emotional impact so that she can get better.[26] Addiction narratives such as those used in twelve-step programs contrast the before and after of recovery and recite a litany of losses associated with addiction, all the while fostering gratitude for recovery. Sam realizes that she has been losing her gratitude for recovery, replacing it with resentment over having the disease.

Samantha has a *slip*, one of several across her journey of recovery. Her ability to admit it to Father Roger means that it does not become a full-blown *relapse*. Father Roger takes several months exploring the slip, inviting her to journal about her state of mind before and after. Most of all, he spends time assuring her that she is not starting over in recovery and helps her build stories about what she values that has emerged from recovery.

The journey of recovery is a long one, almost as long as the journey into addiction. Yet there are reasons for hope. The maintenance and termination stages of recovery do not imply that a person is finished with addiction, but simply that recovery begins to take up more space in life than addiction had. This is not the same as a cure. In recovery, a person needs to catch up on the psychic growth that was stalled throughout the time the addiction was developing.

Why discuss this topic in a section that addresses systems in care? Simply focusing on the person with addiction is not enough, especially when the addiction is fostered in a social world where people are being oppressed and denied opportunities. Pastoral care treatment needs to include advocacy in the social realm. Samantha experiences a pervasive hopelessness in her community, and the reduced cost treatment of Father Roger is part of the ministry of the church that is one of the few addiction treatment options in the area. Social hopelessness is an underacknowledged contributor to addiction.

Using illegal substances fosters a subculture of shared meaning that can separate people from the rest of society. Caring for Samantha's community system means being able to offer drug treatment and prevention early on, along with jobs and other vocational training, to help young people like Samantha see that they have resources to live out their dreams and goals. Surprisingly, new research suggests that giving cocaine addicts cash to help with bills actually leads to a reduction in drug use.[27] In this study, persons with addiction in this situation often use the money for rent rather than for buying drugs, suggesting that even people with serious addiction can be rational when attempting to solve their life problems.[28] It remains to be seen whether the study's results can be replicated, but the insights from the study suggest that it is important to explore social factors in the treatment of addiction.

James is also in a process of maintenance and recovery as a father of someone with addiction. As part of the process, he reaches out to two brothers from whom he had been estranged and attempts to rebuild bridges with them. They judge him for what he is going through with Samantha and have their own problems at home too. Nevertheless, they have a face-to-face exchange where they share their feelings and begin to work through misunderstandings from the past. As Samantha recovers, James begins to explore his own spirituality by becoming involved in a centering prayer group at his parish. In this weekly meeting that forms into an intentional community, he prays and releases his breath, relaxing his own need to control Samantha's addiction, and rediscovering his trust in God. The group becomes a powerful source of friendship whereby everyone cares for its members without blame.

CONCLUSION

Seven percent of the population in the United States is profoundly addicted to alcohol, 2 percent is addicted to illegal drugs, and 5 percent is addicted to gambling. Addiction often accompanies other forms of mental illness such as depression and bipolar disorder.[29] Addiction can be measured along a variety of continua, including frequency of use, harm to a person's relationships, harm to a person's body or mind, the degree of social sanction given to the use of a substance, and a person's motivation to change.[30] All too often addicts are treated like criminals.[31] Here we focus on a paradox in recovery. Treatment for addiction in the United States centers around the criminal justice system that treats addicts as criminals. Yet, for Samantha, because of a dearth of treatment options, the criminal justice system is one of the only ways that she can enter recovery. Rather than being punished with prison, the best approach is multimodal treatment that addresses the multiplicity of risk factors for addiction.

Early on, when substance use is habitual, an intervention can change its course. Later, as the addiction sets in more fully, it approaches the demonic, and its stranglehold can be difficult to break. My own shorthand definition of *addiction* is "when a substance or behavior takes the place of the most important people in one's life, thereby unseating their deeply held ambitions or convictions." This is a progressive process, meaning it can be difficult to pinpoint the exact moment when habitual use becomes abuse.

Yet addiction raises existential questions. For example, Samantha asks Father Roger early in the recovery process, "Does God really love me for who I am?" By supporting her, he shows her that God does accept her. James also begins to trust God's love and rest in it rather than needing to control the outcome of his life.

Although Samantha's addiction had begun with a restlessness longing that echoed God, her habitual search soon turned demonic. Before long, she was violating her own moral compass. Through recovery, she learns what matters again and increases her self-esteem as she is routinely doing things to contribute to the healing of the broader world.

She begins to serve others at a local homeless shelter, helping facilitate an AA meeting for homeless youth. Although Samantha has a criminal record from addiction, she has not yet lost any physical functioning because of her use. In this process, she is moving out of a more egocentric perspective into one where she can see and act on the problems of others. Thankfully, when she stops using, her body immediately begins to heal. In this way she is living more on the path of recovery, becoming more "fully alive," so that her life can demonstrate God's purposes being fulfilled, even amid great pain.

FOR FURTHER REFLECTION

1. What is wrong with the idea that addicts need to hit bottom before they can get help?
2. How do the emotional and spiritual aspects of recovery intersect?
3. What are the consequences of the criminalization of addiction in the United States? What are some alternative approaches that would honor the human person?
4. Why is the twelve-step program such an important source of addiction treatment?

III

CARE
FOR
SELVES

7

THE SANDWICH GENERATION

Denise puts down the phone after calling the pediatrician and sobs. Her tears are ones of exhaustion, not self-pity. Her three-year-old child is home from school with an ear infection. Because Denise's father has entered the middle stages of dementia and can no longer take care of himself, she is trying to find the right care for him. She is also involved in the eucharistic ministry at her church and is behind in her hospital visits. In the middle of it all, she no longer hears the "still small voice" that meant so much early in her faith, a movement in her soul that began when she prayed the Stations of the Cross as a teenager (see 1 Kgs 19:12).

Denise is also living in the "sandwich generation," carrying responsibilities for both young children and elderly parents. All too often the literature in pastoral care focuses on one or the other, as if one was only caring for children or caring for elderly parents. Yet the reality is that many people are caring for both generations, a fact that means they are engaging in constant decision-making, obligations, and caregiving activities within the intimate circle of their own family and the previous generation.

This occurs amid a context where Denise's family has less and less of what they need to get by financially. Since they cannot afford day care, her young children are still a full-time responsibility. In exploring the housing options for her parents, she also finds that the care options for dementia patients are expensive, and she wonders how her family can manage the costs. The financial stresses of the sandwich generation mean that it can be difficult to appreciate what should be generative years of contributing to career and family.[1]

CARE FOR SELVES

Her elderly father has for several years kept careful lists to jog his memory, but nevertheless, in recent months, has fallen behind on bills. The closest daughter and the eldest child, Denise, finds herself drawn into her parents' circle of orbit. As their day-to-day functioning declines, she gets emergency calls directly from her mother when her father begins to wander around the neighborhood. When he gets lost traveling down the street for groceries and leaves a burner on, Denise knows that it is time to intervene and help them plan for the next step. However, her mother continues to deny that her husband is doing badly, fearing the loss of independence that she perceives would come from being "put away."

Caring for her parents is a special burden and responsibility, and many people feel duty bound. Denise feels that she is the one who knows them best. She cherishes their special relationship and has the leeway to give advice and suggestions. Yet as her parents age, she bears a special burden of responsibility. She finds herself saying, "My parents cared for me as a child; now it's my turn to take care of them."[2] The long-established roles and relationships in her family flip, with the care that she has received in the past now becoming part of the care that she is duty bound to give. Her attachment across the generations becomes responsibility.

As she watches her father's health deteriorate, she also feels angry toward her siblings, who are seldom close by to share the day-to-day burdens and joys of such caregiving.[3] This anger is also theological. She realizes that, without knowing it, she thought God might keep her from the senseless suffering of dementia because she has been good. Angry with God, she finds it harder to pray.

Denise's father loses aspects of his social world through the disease. He is no longer able to go to his favorite places and is visited by an ever-shrinking group of friends. Few from the parish seem to recognize that he continues to have spiritual needs despite the dementia. In addition, as a person with dementia, he faces prejudicial attitudes from a highly cognitive and work-oriented society.[4] Even close friends eventually stop visiting because of discomfort, not knowing what to say, and wondering whether their visits make a difference. Denise feels increasingly alone in her caregiving responsibilities. Stressed and without support, she notes how these responsibilities are starting to impact her husband and family.

Caregiving for a family member with dementia is a chronic grieving process since the loved one will never get better. Dementia-related illnesses are devastating because one experiences the chronic loss of memory but also the increased burdens of care, even as the familiar markers of selfhood begin to slip away. Amid such deep loss, some family members might avoid emotional pain by absenting themselves. Denise realizes that she is the "responsible one" in her family and the one who is blamed if something goes wrong in her father's care. It is hard for her to believe that she has any space left to make decisions that mattered to her father, and she seems increasingly stressed by the options that are available to her.

In context, she makes the challenging decision to step away from her father's care briefly to make choices that matter in her own life and faith, clearing some space for reflection and prayer during a season when she can hardly catch her breath.

Now that she is a wife, parent, minister, and daughter in the sandwich generation, she worries she is losing herself in her multiple roles. Everywhere she turns, people ask her to give more. Each of the roles she plays is important. In her role as a eucharistic minister, for example, she feels the satisfaction of being the hands and feet of Christ in the world.

However, to continue doing ministry, Denise must appreciate her own limits, begin to slow down and savor life, and cherish the *person that she is* beyond the roles she plays. As a lay leader and an influential person in her parish, she has a social power inspired by the power of care, yet she feels fatigued by the responsibilities of always caring for others and never having enough time for herself. Thus Denise's caregiving occurs in an interpersonal context where she might experience pain and conflict that she is not fully able to change through transforming systems external to her; she will also need to change herself to interact with these systems with greater wisdom.

Since her own needs are equally important to her family's needs and those whom she serves, it is important that she find ways to share the burden of responsibility so that her needs can be prioritized. She belongs in a network of care. Within this network of caregivers, she may be at a point of high stress when she needs to care for her own needs, experiencing herself as unconditionally loved by God.

THE COURAGEOUS MOVEMENT INTO SILENCE AS SABBATH

Denise packs her bags and goes to a silent retreat at a nearby monastery. She must sacrifice a lot to make the time for herself, as she leaves the children with a bewildered husband and the responsibility for her dementia-ridden father with a younger sister. Reaching out to her relational network for the support she needs, she cannot stop thinking that she is "dropping the ball."

When she checks into the monastery office, she leaves her cell phone there, based on their assurances that if a true emergency arises, her family will contact her through the monastery. For her, releasing the cell phone promises new life, a deepening vitality where she can tune into her heartbeat, her breathing, and herself. More than twice during the retreat she rises suddenly to go to the office and ask for the cell phone, but stops herself, considering her need to return to the silence of the retreat with hopeful peace.

Silent retreats, a practice undertaken at many monasteries and retreat houses, follow formats that include daily prayer, simple meals, and consultation with a spiritual director. A nun responsible for training the retreatants in prayer teaches her the fundamentals of centering prayer, an ancient form that is more of a disposition than a technique.[5]

Halfway through the retreat she remembers a painful childhood memory and shares this with the nun. Simply allowing the memory to come to light and then become a topic of prayer helps tremendously. In the silence she tries to return to the sacred words and pray despite her inevitable wandering thoughts. When it happens, she tries to have compassion on herself, gently returning to the still, small voice that matters so much to her healing.

During prayer in her room, she dwells on a single word or phrase long enough for it to permeate her experience and then rests in the silence. The words on which she reflects are a fragment from her heart, her deepest thoughts and feelings that she cares about the most. Through centered praying, she realizes she has been overwhelmed up until this point, with too many words that are disconnected from a deep source of meaning bombarding her.[6] Again, she feels tears in her eyes, but this time, they are tears of relief and not exhaustion, signals that she is reconnecting with her feeling body and its emotions. In her completely silent retreat, she finds she can care for neglected thoughts and feelings.

She does other activities that contribute to her vitality. Beyond prayer, she hikes in the hills, something she had enjoyed with her father when she was young. She takes a nap in the early afternoon and wakes up to the church bells ringing for prayer followed by a simple meal with the sisters. By taking time for silence, the uninterrupted flow of busy time becomes filled with the peace of a savoring pace, and thus with meaning.

She recognizes that she can no longer deliver the body of Christ to hospitalized patients if she fails to recognize how her own flesh embodies Christ's presence. Indeed, by focusing on her own corporeality as a place where Christ dwells, she begins to understand that care for her own body is the root of the pastoral care that she provides.[7] When she listens to the feelings of others and accepts them, it is possible only because she has first listened with empathy to the experience she is having in her own body. Mindful of the language from chapter 1, Denise is engaging in the practice of attachment, but first attachment to herself. The practice of pastoral care is rooted in specific bodies and reflects God's attachment to us in the body through Jesus Christ.

By learning about her own tendency to overcommit, Denise becomes aware that she has been giving to others without thinking of herself, whereas reorienting through rest helped her realize that her own needs matter as much as the needs of others. Specifically, she can trade her perennially task-oriented self for an opportunity to rest and listen to the promises of God.

INTEGRATING SILENCE AMID CHAOS

Denise experienced the rest of the monastery as a moment of restful peace. Now the challenge is to return to the frantic pace of life and integrate a savoring pace into that busyness. As she returns to the interstate traffic on her way home, she wonders how she will hold on to the silence of the monastic retreat in the complexity of her present situation. How can she return to life in ways that honored her need for inner peace? Given how difficult it is to sustain a savoring pace, Denise realizes that she will need to continue to find a place for rest in a life where she is always responding to others' demands for her time. Deep contemplation inevitably needs to be integrated into the busy nature of everyday life. After she leaves the monastery, she immediately feels stress rise in her neck. While she finds three calls on her cell phone about an emergency at her parents' house, she also learns that her younger sister responded to the crisis by driving three hours to help her parents.

By distancing herself from her obligations, she has created space for others to fill. This sheds new light on her process of discernment, and she finds that she is prepared for everyday schedules of phone conversations with the nursing home, playdates with the neighbors' kids, and her ministry of visitation to the hospital to bring the Eucharist. She finds that the wonder-filled pace of restful time can permeate the week and notes that she is able to live in greater gratitude than previously.

Restful time is set aside where she can meet God without expectation, to wonder and delight in God's presence. When she returns home, she carries a peace that comes from resting in the Spirit. Even her mother-in-law says she looks different. She believes this is because she has experienced an extended rest in God's presence, where she allowed a savoring pace to emerge.

As she returns to her daily routine, Denise decides to quit the church board when her term is up in the spring, devote herself to hospital ministry on Sunday afternoon, and block all church calls for the rest of the week; the pressure to help is sometimes overwhelming. She includes activities for herself in her schedule, such as an art class and a contemplative prayer group at the church. She also decides to take a break from her cell phone from Saturday night until dusk on Sunday, letting it sit silently in the desk drawer. When her activities provoke a "fear of missing out," she attends to the feelings and nourishes them, bathing them with the breath of contemplation rather than fear. It also allows family members to step in and help with the care of her father. By giving everything its own time, she is better able to balance her many commitments rather than constantly responding to emergencies.

She cherishes a few moments of silence at the end of each day, even as she is about to nod off to sleep. In these moments, she meditates on the word *peace* and follows her breath to easily let go of thoughts that come to mind. The experience of contemplation, where she rests in the presence of God, gives her necessary sustenance for the day.

It is not easy for her to negotiate her own self-care with her family. By including her siblings in the network of care, she is no longer solely responsible for her father. In her immediate family, she asks her husband to help with the children more. Despite the conflict that these changes initially require, it is worthwhile prioritizing what she cares about.

Paradoxically, when she rests, Denise can attend to her children in new ways and they respond with joy. She also notes that they connect more deeply with their father while she spends time away from her family. Restful practices of self-care create the conditions in which Denise now feels kept in mind by God, and their children pick up on this. Once she feels kept in mind by God, she can *keep them in mind* by giving them attention, getting on their level, and listening to their voices. She learns that self-care is a prerequisite for the care of children. As noted by Bonnie J. Miller-McLemore, paying attention to children and asking "'What are you going through?' without rushing to give the answer or act on it" is itself a spiritual activity.[8] This ability to pay attention to children is only possible if a caregiver is paying attention to themselves. She also finds she can mediate conflict between her children more easily, taking a deep breath and sharing her own feelings and reasons with them rather than rushing into consequences. Living life at a savoring pace deepens the quality of her parenting.

SPIRITUAL FRIENDSHIP

Denise cannot make all the changes by herself; she needs a mutual friendship with someone who has shared a similar journey. For help, she chooses Joelle, a spiritual director trained in the same model of spiritual direction used at the monastery. Joelle is a busy grandmother who also serves in parish ministry. She knows that Joelle helps take care of her own elderly parents, so she can understand Denise's story.

By talking with Joelle, she can integrate the lessons from the monastery into everyday life, tending to spiritual practices that honor her still, small voice. This allows her to deepen her vocation beyond all the roles that she plays. She also shares the painful childhood memory that had surfaced during the silent retreat and reflects on the difference remembering made in her life as she understands new aspects of herself.

Joelle becomes a "spiritual friend," an *anam cara*, to Denise.[9] The concept is different from a professional relationship with a therapist where behavioral or psychological problems are ameliorated. Rather, spiritual friendship involves cultivating the surrender and joy that is the legacy of the best of the practices of faith. Often the two women end up laughing so hard they are in tears; they feel such kinship from walking the journey of faith together.

Interpersonal relationship is one of the primary arenas where God's presence is revealed. Spiritual mentorship helps people bear their burdens more lightly, discovering glimmering moments of joy and tenacity that provide strength for the journey. Such mentorship relies on the fact that God is already present in Denise's life, in "burning bush" moments of holiness.

People who become mentors in the spiritual life are often those who have experienced some maturity of faith that they then want to pass along to others. Such friends may even help everyday life experiences that might go unacknowledged take on meaning.[10] Being a spiritual friend is like sitting on the aisle seat of a train of spiritual life, while the careseeker is in the window seat reporting on the scenery of life as it passes by.[11]

As a spiritual friend, Joelle's relationship with Denise is an ordinary yet sanctified one. In preparation for each session, Joelle reflects on these questions: "Why me, now?", "*Where is the holy* in Denise's life?" The answer to the first question gives her a clue about how her stories and those of Denise intersect. The answer to the second question fuels holy wonder, the curiosity that helps Joelle become a faithful friend.

Spiritual friendship confers a new identity on the person who chooses the role. This role of spiritual friendship was so important in the early church that monastics received their titles, such as "mother" and "father," from this responsibility.[12] Joelle's expertise in pastoral care and her family experience make her well suited to journey with Denise. It helps that Denise also finds Joelle a pleasing person to be around.

Yet this capacity for spiritual friendship also relies on something deeper: the conviction that, in the holiness of reflecting upon one's life story, a third presence sometimes makes itself known. The third presence manifests itself as a sensation of blessing, a clear call, or a feeling of communion. The third presence is God's unifying reality that makes the everyday responsibilities of interdependence and care lighter.

In her conversations with Joelle, Denise often leaves with a lightened burden, a sense of humor, and a feeling that everything is going to be okay. Through the conversations, she begins to realize her own perfectionism as it has been expressed in her desire to be an ideal mother, daughter, and minister of the church. By allowing someone to minister to her, she begins to release some of the heavy expectations that she has placed on herself. This leads to her opening up to her husband and others about the challenges she is facing, and seeking their help and understanding.

FROM BUSYNESS TO A SAVORING PACE

In our modern times, when asking someone how they are, they invariably answer "busy." This has been called wearing busyness as a badge. It does not seem that people are busier than those who lived in the past, but that people perceive themselves as being busier and maybe even believe that they must be busy. Kirk Byron Jones examines what we miss by moving rapidly from one thing to another. He asks, "Why do we run?" and his answers include, among others, to be "in control," "to please people," or "to get our share."[13] In addition to these psychological reasons, there are also practical concerns, such as Denise's experience of caregiving.

Behind each of these reasons for running is a psychological motivation and a theological belief—a belief about God's nature and response to humanity. Psychologically, people might engage a false self to be perfect, thereby missing their calling and forsaking some part of their distinctive identity. Theologically, busyness may be a way of attempting to please God by using good works to hide the authentic self. Ministers, who are taught as children to meet the needs of others, continue to do so as adults, even at some cost to themselves.[14]

By slowing down time and resting in the gift of awareness that comes from God's creative rest, the practice of Sabbath offers an experience of peace and reflection in which one can examine the deeper self. Ministers never engage in ministry from pure motives, but always with a mixture of altruism and ego aggrandizement. In times of trial, the mixture of motives comes to the surface. When ministry lacks emotional or spiritual rewards, it can be hard to cope with the day-to-day activity.[15] If ministers continue without insight into their given ways of operating, they might burn out or harm those in their care, since they are functioning from their "unseen-unseeing self."[16] Just as people can be "unaware of their personal condition" as they go on caring for others, such busyness can finally eventuate in "soul abuse" as ministers lose touch with themselves.[17] Soul abuse appears when a person neglects their own needs to the point of violation of personhood, all for the sake of caring for others.

Sabbath gives people a chance to see what is hidden underneath their everyday lives. Facing this hidden pain, Jones argues, allows ministers to put their own personhood before their ministry. Some ministers may serve others out of a sense of emptiness: "If I play this role, I will be filled up;" other ministers may engage in kind acts and respond with anger when their gifts are not acknowledged: "Why can't people appreciate the role that I play?" Some ministers may feel overwhelmed by the psychic pain of their community that is suffering from social problems such as unemployment or addiction. Recognizing one's personal response to reaching limits, and the unconscious expectations that ministers hold when they reach their own limits, is helpful for self-growth.

Advocates for social justice can sometimes be overwhelmed by the busyness of their work, rushing from one event to another. Martin Luther King Jr., in the days of the Montgomery bus boycott, complained about "the frustration of feeling in the midst of so many things to do I am not doing anything well."[18] The feeling of frustration is compounded when the person seems unable to change their circumstances. Caregivers and advocates like these are on the frontlines of human suffering in their day-to-day work. Both feel the fatigue of constantly responding to this suffering and may long for a chance to experience peace.

Fully embodied personhood is an antidote to the futility that comes from burnout and its attendant despair. For Jones, human personhood comes before activity. One way to experience personhood is to slow down to encounter the self fully. It is likely that, in living out roles, people become busier and lose touch with their own senses. In contrast to mindlessly traveling through the day, *ministers can slow their pace, savor sight and sound, and meditate on that which brings gratitude.*[19]

Jones calls this living "at a savoring pace," an approach that will lead to new wholeness and a more fruitful vision for ministry. An initial step toward savoring is dwelling on sensory experience. This requires a moment of emptiness. For example, Mother Theresa stated, "Listen in silence, because if your heart is full of other things it cannot hear the voice of God."[20] In order to have a self through which to reclaim the senses and savor experience, a person needs to experience selfhood as a gift from God. The savoring pace always comes as a gift from God and often takes negotiation and effort to accomplish. A savoring pace requires stopping long enough to listen and then attending to the activity of life once this activity is resumed. God's purposes are worked out in a minister's attention to the ordinary.

In the field of pastoral care, it is especially tempting to exchange the opportunity for self-reflection with another good work that needs to be done. The constant demands of pastoral work mean that there will always be someone whose needs something from the minister. Pastoral care involves the balancing act of commitments to oneself, one's family, and others' suffering. Within a religious community, as in others, there are multiple competing demands that must be assessed. Amid all this busyness, it is important to stand still as Adam and Eve did in the Garden of Eden, allowing God to call out their names.[21] The start of self-care is simply slowing down enough to be found by God.

On a fundamental level, Denise is not sure if she is seen or heard by God and wants to serve others as a way of feeling close to God. Her primary motivation is not arrogance but insufficiency. If she is haunted by anything, it is the fear that she is not giving enough rather than her "hopeful" pride.[22] What Denise realizes through the practice of Sabbath, however, is that God does indeed see her. In fact, God spreads this tent of peace over her so that she can rest in her body and return to vital contact with her spirit.

By learning to rest in this way, Denise establishes better boundaries so that she can decide how she wants to and when she is ready to respond to demands from the parish and other volunteer opportunities. By deciding when she is ready, she can determine how to serve and thus give herself entirely to each new task. It allows her to build in a moment of rest before she responds to the next call and makes an important self-care decision. This means that when she responds to a call she feels truly ready to do so.

SELF-CARE AS A THEOLOGICAL ACT

Care for the self invites the use of theological discernment; self-knowledge requires knowing God. As John Calvin, at the outset of his book *Institutes of the Christian Religion*, states, "Nearly all the wisdom we possess, that is to say, true and sound wisdom, consists of two parts, the knowledge of God and of ourselves...which one precedes and brings forth the other is not easy to discern."[23] Knowing a little about psychology can actually aid in the knowledge of God; likewise, knowing some theology can help understand people's motivations.

It is important that caregivers trust in a provident God who, despite life's mysteries, is present and actively working toward the good.

Knowing that God loves us and is involved in the world allows ministers to join where God is already acting rather than rushing in to take his place. Those who operate in a rush often feel that they must do everything because God's kingdom of peace and justice is up to them. Yet, because God's care comes first, ministers can engage in their work with the peace of knowing that God is active. How one does pastoral care is equally important to what one does, and a restful pace of pastoral care comes from knowing that God is present in the world working for the good.

In addition to important ministry priorities at the parish, Denise is also responsible for care of specific people in her family who depend on her. She needs to negotiate, through a process of discernment, what care comes first, since she is too busy to do everything. God is already at work through Denise's life and ministry, so discernment means discovering where God is present, already creating a peaceful place for her, and dwelling where God is fully present in her life.

By slowing down and attending to her emotions and her body, Denise may discover spiritual practices that have sustained her in the past and become more insightful about her life in the process.[24] These practices create conditions for self-awareness, introducing a moment of rest that shifts an otherwise chaotic and overwhelming schedule. By becoming aware of her thoughts and feelings, Denise can meditate on herself as being created in the image of God. Pondering her experience means learning to value her personhood over the roles that she plays.[25]

God's unconditional love for Denise is the first and most important thing. Whatever ministry she does flows from this love, making it possible and giving it richness and depth. The lived experience of God's love is like a deep well of inexhaustible riches. It is not easy to grasp, but it can be humbling to touch this profound love. Tapping into the experience helps her flourish and make decisions about self-care.

Denise is feeling so overwhelmed by the demands in her life that she sometimes feels like things are futile. One of the best ways to treat the feeling that one is just playing out a role is to reclaim the practice of Sabbath. Sabbath is a grace-filled response to God's gift of time in which God sets up the conditions of peace and invites us to listen and rest in response. It is not another job to do, but rather a reflection of God at work in the world, doing what is impossible for people to do.

Denise has been taught to give to others ever since she was young. This is problematic now because she tends to overcommit and then feel disoriented and unsettled as she tries to meet life's many demands. God wants to reflect God's glory through her and this does not require that she unconditionally sacrifice herself for others. Rather, sympathy, compassion, and kindness to herself are among the primary virtues that she needs to cultivate at this moment.

By becoming aware of God's unconditional love, she embraces the possibilities and richness of her ministry. At this point in her life, God wishes to place, in the words of a Sabbath prayer, "a tent of peace" over Denise, so that she can experience the restoration and health that allow for creative thriving.[26] Her busyness is not sinful. She is balancing multiple goods, intrinsic and vital elements of life lived well, that each demand her time. Nevertheless, when she slows down, she experiences a shift that allows her to experience these demands differently.

God invites her to experience God's love for her without mediation; God reaches out to her and calls for her response. This is not an issue of salvation—Christ's act on the behalf of humanity—but rather an aspect of sanctification, learning to live more fully into the life God wishes for her. This belongs in sanctification, that area where God fosters human flourishing and fulfillment, rather than justification.

Sabbath is a place where Denise can redeem time. By resting on the seventh day, God adds something to the world, a sense of grateful joy and peaceful re-creation that is a part of her faithful reaction to God's mercy. All too often Christians feel they must be productive in response to God's gift of grace, but they are invited to the experience of Sabbath where they rest and listen to God's voice. In her response of restful quiet, Denise can imitate such joyful re-creation. God's gift to Denise is to help her remember that her embodied self matters and that God delights in her regardless of what she can do or accomplish.

CONCLUSION

In a moment of despair in which Denise meets her own limits, she cries out to God. In the sandwich generation—those who care for children and elderly parents—she understands that she carries burdens of stress and responsibility that come from her sibling position, her relationships to her parents, children, and others. She faces a hallmark of burnout, a disrupted spirituality in which life's meaning is starting to dissipate.

Busyness is a chief condition of modern life, nearly a badge of honor for many. Denise truly *is* busy, all that she does are significant goods, in and of themselves. Yet it is time for her to include care for her own personhood as a priority in addition to care for others. The fundamental truth of the Christian life, that God loves each minister regardless of what they can perform or accomplish, became a reality in her life when she slowed down and reflected.

Denise is going through one of life's most difficult transitions in which she begins to be a caregiver for elderly parents that need help while also caring for her children and family. Often arising from a sense of obligation— "I need to provide care for my parents because they cared for me as a child"—she notices that dementia led to a progressive shrinking of the social world around her father. Because she is the oldest sibling, she takes on much responsibility for work, and she feels the fatigue of mind and spirit as a result.

While being torn in multiple directions, feeling both that her family needs her and that her own faith was becoming more distant, Denise enters the respite of Sabbath, God's gift of restful and re-creating time. Sabbath means that God places a "tent of peace" over Denise when she can no longer care for herself. This gift of Sabbath slows her down to embrace a different rhythm. The savoring pace begins with the wisdom of her senses and moves outward so that she can fully experience life's richness.

Observing the Sabbath away from her duties, Denise learned about the practice of centering prayer. She also invited a spiritual friend into her life and honored an ancient model of soul friendship that helps bless everyday life and make meaning of experience. Her soul friend, also a parent and a caregiver, could understand the multiple demands that Denise was facing. Through soul friendship, she discovered that God was present in the holy ground of her busy life. The knowledge helped her set new limits in her parish ministry, with caregiving for her father, and in parenting, to do all these activities with more focus and intention. Denise slowly realized at a deep experiential level that God loves her regardless of what she can do or perform. The service she gives comes from the deep awareness of God's unconditional love for her, allowing her to rest even as she carried on with her busy daily activities.

FOR FURTHER REFLECTION

1. How is Sabbath different from self-help?
2. What causes a minister such as Denise stress?
3. How did Denise use the silent retreat, and what difference did it make in her life?
4. How does spiritual friendship help stressed caregivers continue to deepen their ministry?
5. What could be done for overworked ministers so that they could experience Sabbath?

8

STORIES OF CREATING BOUNDARIES

Father George is very kind, pastoral, and well admired by all his parishioners, especially the women in the church. He frequently hears confessions on Saturday morning and then follows up with home visits. When people come to him for counseling, he asks them how they are doing with their specific difficulties.

Patricia, a recent divorcée with questions about the church's stance, pours out her heart to Father George in pastoral visits. In his mind he tells himself that he is becoming significant to her. He cares for her story with depth and feeling. He thinks of it as a pastoral relationship that matters, and yet he finds himself looking forward to their meetings on a personal level. Important lay leaders begin to resent the special relationship that is forming between Father George and Patricia.

Within a few months, when he loses his father suddenly and is deeply shaken, he reaches out to Patricia and asks to meet her. During their rendezvous, he tells her how he is attracted to her. He follows up with an explicit text message after their meeting. Now, in addition to crossing the emotional threshold, sexual boundaries are breached. Although he usually trusts his feelings, in this instance, Father George realizes at a gut level that this will end badly. Through the church's intervention it becomes clear that they can no longer meet. Patricia feels devastated and wonders if she can ever trust him again. She has already lost her priest; if she follows up with accusations about him, she could lose her parish as well. At the same time, unable to grapple with his own responsibility, he blames *her* for the event and threatens that if she ever tells anyone, she will be exiled from the community.

INSTITUTIONAL RESPONSES

Patricia does tell a capable bishop whom she knows through a family connection. The bishop's office responds immediately by starting an investigation. This investigation and disclosure are an important aspect of helping the community cope after the trauma of a ministerial boundary violation.

Because he had experience in dealing with the ongoing child sexual abuse crisis, the bishop pursues the report of Father George's purported sexual harassment seriously, with the aim of investigating and healing the community utmost in his mind rather than silencing the victim.

The bishop finds out what other women Father George might have counseled and whether sexual liberties may have been taken or emotional lines crossed. If it is a pattern, it must mean immediate removal of Father George from his ministry post for counseling and a full disclosure to the community of faith. By being defrocked immediately, rather than being moved to another parish, region, or type of ministry, the church assures that ministry continues to be wise and faithful stewardship of stories rather than the harm of the flock for the sake of secrecy and complicity.[1] Although the church sometimes removes priests without defrocking them, if the priest has shown a pattern of abuse, it can be difficult to correct this behavior and defrocking is the more appropriate response.

The bishop knows that it is important to work with other lay leaders to disclose what happens in the church and help them process their feelings related to the events.[2] After an instance of potential boundary violation, a team from the parish needs to be equipped to disclose what is found and describe how it is being investigated, with the aim of the full pastoral healing of the community. The disclosure process, which ideally takes at least four hours, is undertaken by the religious community's own trusted leaders.[3]

It is important for the health of a religious community that a disclosure of the abuse take place in a safe holding environment where people can share their questions and concerns as soon as possible. A secure environment is one where people can talk in small groups and express the full range of emotions. The event should include a presentation by a lay leader who has received training in the phenomenon of the clergy abuse of power. It should also include a necessary time for breakout sessions where small groups can share their feelings with trained facilitators. The leader avoids calling it adultery or a fling and uses the language of betrayal of pastoral trust. Throughout the process of disclosure, the facilitators must also avoid saying "no comment." Instead, they should describe what they can and, while limited in sharing their knowledge of a specific case—such as ongoing litigation— give as much information as possible to those involved and share their thinking with those gathered.

Some parishioners deny any allegations, blame victims, and otherwise choose to resist the process. Such moments of pushback are expected, and a full and honest disclosure process can prevent emotional conflict from derailing the religious community. Welcoming these difficult emotions in a faith context is a sign of the religious community's vitality.

Too often, religious communities skip the necessary step of disclosure because it seems too painful, and they imagine that time will heal the wounds. They live with the undercurrents of secrecy and abuse for decades. These secrets impact all ministers who come after the abuse. Even people who are not close to the pastor or the victim need a transparent disclosure process that attends to everyone's feelings.

Healthy disclosure is part of the religious community's mission since it gives a tone of frank and open faith that allows people to heal from what is really happening in their lives together. Indeed, someone who had experienced sexual harassment in the workplace might enter the religious community at the time of disclosure and be inspired by how the religious community confronts the problem head on rather than protecting the abuser as often happens with powerful people in the secular world.

After the parish laical commission does its work of disclosure, this parish is riven with conflict for a time. Many take Father George's side and blame Patricia; others demand that he pay a severe legal penalty and lose his ministry. Many parishioners focus on the priest's needs rather than Patricia's.

Father George is removed from his post and enters counseling, where he becomes aware of some of the warning signs that he should have spotted in ministry. He understands his own reactions to the pain of others and how it creates a false intimacy with them, and practices setting better boundaries and meeting needs in his personal life. Father George begins creating such healthy boundaries by not allowing parishioners to be part of his private social media accounts.

In consultation with his counselor, synod leaders decide that Father George is healthy enough to enter a new parish. They are given a ministry team that helps them make the transition. To make their determination, they consult with a neutral outside counselor not affiliated with the church who determines that he is becoming more self-aware and shows potential for further self-growth. This means he can learn from his mistakes and he is capable through counseling and supervision to see some of his blind spots and change the activity that led to the abuse. He is also assigned to further counseling in his new post with a mentor outside the ecclesial system who can alert the authorities if they see any risk of continued boundary violations. He is not allowed to retain ties with this old parish in any form.

In his new parish, Father George is frank about his mistakes in the past and uses his experience to make sure that his parishioners learn about boundaries and setting limits in the parish's life. Likewise, bishops and other institutional authorities talk about the steps they take to make sure that Father George's new community is safe. They instate a "safe touch" program for children and help parishioners know how to establish appropriate boundaries in pastoral care.[4]

Patricia leaves the parish and enters counseling with a trauma therapist who has worked with clergy sexual harassment victims. She spends time restoring her perceptions and coming to believe that what she experienced was wrong.[5] While her faith is deeply shaken, she retains a trust in God, even while she becomes more suspicious of ecclesiastical authority. As part of her healing she eventually takes action by establishing a nonprofit organization committed to addressing the abuse of power by ministers and other religious professionals and writes in the field of pastoral ethics that offers an ethical framework for ministry.

VULNERABILITY IN THE CARE FOR STORIES: WINDOWS AND WALLS

The work of pastoral care and counseling engages vulnerability, and when people are vulnerable, there is a risk of boundary violations.

CARE FOR SELVES

Ministry is a sacred space in which to hear stories. This has been symbolized in religious practices such as the confessional and can even be glimpsed in the pastoral counseling session. Father George often heard confessions, and, as much as he tried not to, he remembered people's stories. His challenge was to keep the sacred trust that is given to him by not sharing stories with others or use what he learned to take advantage of the vulnerability that comes from hearing their deep needs. Ministerial counseling is closely related in its presumed confidentiality, the proper boundaries around it, and the healthy self-care of the minister.

Lay and ordained ministers alike gain power through counseling. In Father George's case, he received access to Patricia because she shared the details of a painful divorce with him in the context of exploring the church's position that divorced persons cannot partake in the sacrament. In explaining the theological meaning of divorce he is not examining an issue that is neutral to Patricia, but one that matters to her heart and soul. Therefore, when he confirmed how God accepts her, he gave her a message that was a relief to her. Because this question is weighted with much theological baggage and questions of self-acceptance, discussion of the matter makes her vulnerable to him.

Father George was called to keep a sacred trust and to honor her vulnerability in the presence of God. He could do this if he cared for his own stories, his loneliness, and the pain of his recent loss. Since he did not care for his own story adequately, he became manipulative in his work and interpreted her vulnerability as signs of sexual availability. He had a pattern of turning difficult feelings in his own life into sexual ones and trusting these intuitions to tell him how to act.[6]

In other words, Father George's relationship with Patricia was an unequal power relationship in which he exploited her vulnerabilities to meet his own needs. The fact that he is not aware of exploiting her vulnerability does not relieve him of ethical responsibility. Ministry always comes from a situation of unequal power. In pastoral ministry, the professional power is heightened when a minister builds trust, travels with people along their journeys, and symbolizes God to them. The fact that absolute strangers share their problems with ministers indicates the imbalance of pastoral power. Ministry is a place of vulnerability, as it requires caring for stories that connect with needs of attachment, time, context, and meaning-making.

To better understand this phenomenon, it is helpful to draw from

118

a metaphor from the marriage counseling literature. Spouses and those in intimate partnerships are supposed to have windows between them so that they can communicate freely but walls to those outside the relationship that keep key information private to the marital relationship. This means that there will be private things that belong only in the sanctity of one's most intimate relationships. With proper windows and walls, couples can share with each other freely, respond to each other's invitations to emotional intimacy, and sustain the proper boundaries to protect their relationship from outsiders.[7]

Yet some people come to a religious community without any walls around their marriage and seek intimacy from a minister. Likewise, ministers may feel "married" to their work, and for this reason they might assume that parishioners are there to meet their own emotional needs as equals. Celibate ministers may lack close friends. If they live in a competitive religious culture, they may believe that they have no one with whom to communicate openly and may instead rely upon parishioners for intimacy needs, feeling an odd sort of satisfaction when they can hear the specific details of a person's painful past. Ministers need walls between their personal life and their relationships with parishioners to stay healthy, and boundaries of space and time that help them keep the work they do sacred and separate from their personal lives.

Lay leaders need to have a chance to return to intimate relationships in their own lives rather than trying to meet intimacy needs through parishioners. Ministers need to get emotional needs met among peers. Mixing lonely clergy and lay leaders with conflicted marriages can create conditions in which emotional affairs and other forms of boundary crossing occur.[8]

If ministers begin to look forward to specific relationships in the parish while keeping details of them private from their superiors, they need better walls in their ministry. Lay leaders can notice if many of their most important relationships occur among the church staff rather than with their own families and readjust their boundaries accordingly. Special relationships between a minister and a family in the parish can lead to conflict as others wonder why the family has been chosen as special friends.

Because they represent that which is most holy, ministers must be careful to guard the boundaries of their own windows and walls to protect the fragile and precious story care that is the sacred task of ministry.

Ordained clergy lead in worship, guide the congregation or parish, and foster the community's gathered life. Lay ministers create educational and service opportunities and deliver the sacraments to those in need. Ministry creates a form of intimacy that can challenge people's walls.

Yet the intimacy does not flow equally well between ministers and parishioners. It is the responsibility of ministers to manage boundaries, even with those who lack clear ones themselves, to continue to guard the religious community's sacred trust. For the care for stories to remain sacred, people need to believe that their minister does not need them for emotional or sexual gratification.[9]

It is helpful to give some initial definitions. Sexual harassment includes the use of lewd or demeaning references or pictures in office spaces, as in a text message. Sexual assault occurs when a minister uses others for sexual gratification, touching in inappropriate ways. In small communities, giving and receiving favors, gifts, or discounts can be a prelude to later boundary violations or hidden expectations, and ministers need to be trained to say "no thank you," to "small" gifts because they cannot always see the deeper intention behind the gift. These boundary violations are a *misuse of pastoral power* since they betray the trust of the office. Rather than an affair or a fling, they exploit the inevitable inequality of power between ministers and their parishioners.[10]

It is an emotional affair when someone has replaced a spouse or partner with a confidante outside the relationship who is perceived to be better than one's spouse. For celibate clerics and religious sisters, an emotional affair can happen when a significant parishioner takes the place of their religious community. Emotional affairs are secret and rely upon the notion that the new person will replace what is lacking in one's intimate relationship.[11] Emotional affairs are just as detrimental to religious communities as sexual ones since they create a feeling of specialness with one and a lack of clarity among everyone else.

BOUNDARIES IN CHURCH

To have a boundary is to be limited in some sense; in another sense, a boundary is based on the root word *bound*, meaning "to leap or jump."[12] Paradoxically, the word *boundary* indicates both limits and the capacity for joyful freedom since both offer the opportunity for proper pastoral relationship.

In the Catholic denomination, there is a clear boundary against sexual relationships. Of course, sexual abuse of minors is never permissible. Yet, even in Protestant denominations, ministers cannot have sexual or romantic relationships with parishioners, simply because it will not work. They destroy the pastoral relationship for the parishioner who becomes involved and create toxic emotional undercurrents in congregations, with people asking themselves, "Why wasn't I chosen by the pastor?" Such relationships foster favoritism and secrets that erode the trust of a community and constitute a misuse of power.

Sexual and emotional relationships between ministers and parishioners or staff people at the church, even if they are adult relationships, destroy the attachment aspect of story care on the communal level. Appropriate attachment builds a sense of safety and belonging; the secrets and misuse of power in such relationships erode safety and create a sense of violation for the whole fellowship.

In the past, Protestant congregants often wanted to match their unmarried pastor with an available son or daughter of the congregation. Such arrangements are seldom effective because special relationships create favoritism. By caring for stories in ways that honor attachment, time, context, and meaning-making, ministers sustain the fragile intimacy that is part of the freedom of the pastoral office, an intimacy that must not be damaged through sexual or emotional boundary crossing or special relationships that show favoritism.

The responsibility to maintain boundaries remains solely with the minister. It is important not to follow the priest's example and blame Patricia for her relationship with Father George. Patricia is not a seductress nor a temptress. Even if she had initiated a relationship with him, he is responsible to safeguard the sanctity of her story. Ministers who only trust their own instincts in counseling, rather than getting supervision, can inappropriately sexualize pastoral relationships.[13]

THE PARADOX OF PASTORAL POWER

Ministry is a sacred task in which people attempt to help others glorify God and walk in faith, fostering intimacy between the parishioner and themselves. Pastoral counseling can lead through broken, vulnerable places. People who share difficult events and feelings with ministers frequently feel closer to the minister; they have their emotional needs met through a pastoral relationship. With Father George and Patricia, it was not an equal relationship. Ministers cannot depend upon parishioners to feel close to them. Instead, it is important to remember that pastoral relationships are always for the sake of parishioners to safeguard the sanctity of the ministerial office.

The intimacy is never meant *for* the minister. Ministers stand for what is holy, for the horizon of what matters most. This can be seen when people reach out to the minister for advice or support simply because the minister is associated with the church. Even in pastoral counseling at a clinic, a person is frequently sought because she is an ordained minister and can help integrate spiritual life by addressing psychological problems.

Being clear about the difference between pastoral care, counseling, and mutual friendships is an important ministerial skill. As noted, ministry need not meet a minister's primary needs for friendship and communion. Mutual friendships can be difficult between ministers and their parishioners because the office of ministry is always in the background. Ministry is a practice of leading people to deepen their relationship with God and supporting them in their life of faith.

Some ministers are uncomfortable with their office, with the idea that they have real authority. They express uncertainty about the fact that people trust them to guide their spiritual lives. Other ministers feel uncomfortable with the trust placed in them because of their public roles. They might use the discomfort with their office to be like everyone else, sharing bawdy jokes to show that they are just "one of the guys" and risk crossing boundaries. Conversely, they might share some of their doubts or mistakes with those in their care, asking their parishioners to help them along. Instead, ministers need to be aware that in the act of trying to diminish their office, they create more conditions for boundary violations to occur.

When pastoral caregivers hear those in their care say, "I wish I had faith like yours," they might be tempted to diminish these comments and share some of their own difficulties in the mistaken belief that they can then make things more equitable with those in their care. When parishioners transfer powerful feelings to a minister, it is best to accept them and honor the relationship rather than challenge them.[14] The best way to use transferences is to recognize and honor them as a place where God is at work. By accepting a compliment and simply saying, "Thank you," rather than saying, "I'm just a sinner like you," a minister can honor what they mean to a parishioner. By honoring this, they keep the professional boundaries of the relationship in place.

If a minister hears a confidential disclosure in a pastoral counseling setting and immediately goes on to disclose something from her own life in the session, it does not help the careseeker, but is, in fact, a sign that a boundary might be crossed soon. A minister does not get rid of authority by downplaying the ministerial role. It does not work to even the playing field. They paradoxically *heighten* their authority because it gives them more access and power in people's lives.

LEARNING TO BE SIGNIFICANT, NOT SPECIAL

Many psychological factors may lead clergy to cross sexual boundaries. Research has shown that a minister who has low self-esteem and pours everything into their work, while having unrealistic expectations about ministerial authority, may be more likely to cross a sexual boundary, including sexual abuse.

Clericalism is the idea that someone is special because of their ordination. This idea has been associated with a higher incidence of sexual abuse because it creates awe around the minister. The inordinate fear and respect accorded the clergy under clericalism makes it difficult for survivors to acknowledge their sexual abuse and heal from it, and for the institution to respond properly by investigating and punishing the abuser.[15]

Father George alternated between a very high view of his office—the priestly function matters a great deal to him—and a very low self-image. Therefore, he was at a greater risk for boundary violations than someone who believed that laypeople have equal status before God.[16] Likewise, Patricia may have implicitly trusted Father George because his religious authority obscured his manipulative behavior.

Some ministers feel special because of the work they do. They sense that they are chosen by God and have a very clear role to play in helping bring about God's work of salvation in the world. Other ministers feel completely unworthy and emphasize that they are only meant to be tools in God's hands. Father George had elements of both. These twin beliefs can be dangerous because they imply both a grandiosity and a shame, two sides of the same coin.[17] An overly humble persona shows false humility, or shameful narcissism, which becomes a way of trying to boost one's power through denying it. By constantly downplaying their importance, they make people feel sorry for them and care for them. The strategy in fact heightens one's power over those one serves.

Ministers are not special because of the role they serve, yet they are significant before God just as every other person is significant. When ministers understand that they are *significant* rather than special, they can be realistic about their importance in the lives of the people for whom they care and recognize that, in each instance, the pastoral relationship is meant *for the care* of parishioners rather than for the minister's own needs. Ministry that is *significant and not special, grounded in communities of support and supervision,* is less likely to cross boundaries in their parish.

The ultimate corrective to shameful narcissism is a proper understanding of one's worth before God. God makes ministry significant and grounds the approach to it. A minister who feels significant because of God's love for them seems comfortable in their own skin. They also are aware of how important the ministry of story care is to others, so they are careful to guard it rather than misuse it.

Reconnecting with place, family, and context can help ministers become significant rather than special. Even ordained ministers are, first, church members who come from specific places. Some ministers leave their families early, never returning for holidays, and they may need to be encouraged to return home and discover their home place.[18] Expectations and even hostility can be signs that ministers matter to their people. By engaging in self-exploration, ministers can become strong enough to face these emotional dynamics.

Being grounded in a community of support and supervision means one knows where to turn for help and is not afraid of being penalized for asking for assistance in complicated situations. In competitive church cultures where there are secretive processes of discipline, people frequently hold back from asking for help because they believe they will be penalized. This culture risks higher rates of boundary crossing among their ministers.

Honoring one's office requires self-awareness. The second chapter claimed that ministry is often rooted in unmet childhood needs that need to be addressed through exploration of one's unconscious expectations and needs. Paradoxically, one only becomes self-aware through community with others, having someone name the unconscious behaviors that are being acted out. This can happen in counseling, spiritual direction, or clinical pastoral education, where ministers can learn blind spots and become aware of growing edges.[19] The ability to be significant to someone else builds on early attachment strengths such as a feeling of belonging and an ability to take risks.

Ministers in these communities need creative ways to access communities of support that can help them build on their knowledge. Communities of support for ministers include networks of referral, such as counselors who understand specialized issues of trauma and abuse. It is also important to develop relationships with friends and mentors who can give strength for the journey. They can help ministers to let their hair down and find a place where they can be themselves without anything to prove.

Communities of supervision grant the scope to one's ministry by evaluating whether one is staying within the range of one's appropriate practice and helping ministers to get additional training. These communities should have disciplinary authority over ministers. This is more than stepping in when misconduct is happening, but it is about helping people become the best they can and to work within their religious community's guidelines for best practice.[20] Rather than going it alone, a supervised minister has the freedom to do ministry and is equipped for the difficult tasks ahead.

In the previous chapter, Denise experienced a deeper insight into some ways that she could create helpful boundaries that would help her sustain a savoring pace amid her busy life. Through spiritual direction, the counseling worked well because her spiritual director could see behaviors that Denise could not see for herself. In clinical pastoral education, seminary students can also see their own growing edges within a supportive community as they share verbatims on difficult pastoral care scenarios.

People do not grow into self-awareness overnight. For some, there are limits to self-awareness, and these persons should not minister with vulnerable parishioners. Self-awareness occurs most readily in communities that offer a great deal of education as well as clear boundaries, as these communities foster a sense of safety. The greater amount of safety a community provides—self-awareness, the right kinds of responsibility and expectations, and healthy interactions—the more ministers will be able to risk as they grow into their pastoral roles.

CONFIDENTIAL SPEECH AND ITS LIMITS

Sexual and emotional boundary violations are not the only areas where the trust of the pastoral office can be violated. To understand the dynamics of confidentiality, we consider another brief story that explains the importance of confidentiality and how easily it can be broken.[21]

A deacon visits a patient in the hospital and later sees her sister in the elevator. The deacon shares the story of how he had just visited the patient and brought her the Eucharist. The patient is furious because she is in the hospital for a private procedure and the deacon has violated her confidentiality by sharing that she is in the hospital. This story reminds us that anything that happens in a hospital must be kept confidential unless explicit permission is received from a patient to share it.

In ministry with adults in the church, there is a strong presumption of confidentiality that should not be taken lightly. However, there are times when a person's emotional and physical well-being come before their need for confidentiality. In these cases where people might be a danger to themselves or others, a minister needs to break confidentiality and report the allegations of abuse to the right authorities. Ministers are mandatory reporters if they suspect the abuse of children, the elderly, or the disabled. They report in consultation with their colleagues in ministry.

In cases where there is the risk of harm to oneself or others, the presumption of confidentiality no longer pertains, and clergy become mandated reporters according to the guidelines of the state in which they work.[22] It takes time, wisdom, and discernment to become adept at knowing how to break confidentiality, often in consultation with supervisors. Ministers need to know the protections of confidential speech pertaining to their ministry roles in the states that they serve. Confidentiality should not be inadvertently or wrongly broken, and ministers must always safeguard the trust placed on them in pastoral care.

If they sense they are about to receive the disclosure of abuse or misconduct, they need to let a person know that if they disclose the potential to harm oneself or others, then they may need to make a report to an outside agency to get needed help. In all instances, the harmed person needs to be alerted that ministerial confidentiality must be broken, and steps can be taken to accompany them in this process. There are some secrets that a minister cannot keep. Sometimes the process of investigation is the beginning of a healing journey for a family and their parish.

Many ministers need help in setting confidential boundaries. One parish associate heard a lot of gossipy conversations about their priest from parishioners. Through a training on family systems and healthy communication, the parish associate learned that it is important to encourage parishioners to approach the priest directly with their concerns rather than trying to funnel them through her.[23] Engaging in the whispers about people who are in leadership can foster conflict within a community. At the same time, priests and senior ministers benefit from honest and confidential supervision to become more effective leaders through becoming aware of their own unseen patterns.

The privileged communication of the confessional is the strongest form of privacy, inviolate against the law in many states, and there is nothing else like it in pastoral ministry. Yet, in some communities, even the confessional is not protected from legal inquiry. It is important for ministers to research their own state's laws about confidentiality and mandatory reporting to determine when they need to break presumed confidentiality for the greater good.

CONCLUSION

Sexual and emotional misconduct or abuse in religious communities occurs when ministers of any kind engage in sexual relationships or emotional affairs with their parishioners. These boundary violations are a *misuse of pastoral power* since they betray the trust of the office. Rather than an affair or a fling, they exploit the inevitable inequality of power between ministers and their parishioners.[24]

The dynamics of power mean that when a minister turns to a parishioner to meet unspoken psychological, sexual, or social needs, a minister violates pastoral office, which must be maintained solely for the sake of the parishioner.

If a minister spends a great deal of time counseling vulnerable members in private situations without proper supervision, they are at risk for boundary violations. One sign of a potential boundary violation is extensive self-disclosure by the minister in a counseling scenario.

Likewise, ministers need to have friends and family outside the congregation that they rely on for support so that they do not turn to their parishioners as confidants.

After a minister has abused pastoral office, there needs to be disclosure. This occurs through crisis ministry that clearly identifies the harm done and safeguards the needs of survivors first. Then, the leadership can address the entire community's need to heal through frank conversation and cooperative care.

Full disclosure is especially important in helping congregants move into the future, understanding and normalizing their perceptions and feelings. Disclosure sessions are done best if a congregation also has a clear policy in place for dealing with perpetrators. The policy needs to include specific guidelines to keep judiciaries from moving abusers from one congregation to another.[25]

Regardless of a minister's specific vocation—a lay leader, parish associate, chaplain, or religious educator—ministry confers a power that comes from caring for stories. Safeguarding their power means having a realistic understanding of it. Ministers cannot have sexual or romantic relationships with people in their congregation, and they need friends and family outside the church where they serve—thus caring for their own stories—rather than emotional entanglements with their parishioners.

FOR FURTHER REFLECTION

1. Why does ministry have a high rate of sexual and emotional boundary crossing?
2. Does it decrease a minister's power for a minister to downplay the authority of their office to be like everyone else? Why or why not?
3. What is confidentiality in pastoral care and what are its limits? How would you break confidentiality if you realized that someone was a danger to themselves or others?

CONCLUSION
A Theology for Hopeful Caring

Instead of goal-driven, outcomes-based therapy, pastoral care and counseling is attuned to a suffering person's need for partnership. The problems in today's world are too complex for simple formulas. When ministers provide pastoral care, they are on the frontlines of a variety of forms of psychological suffering impacted by social context, and they engage these sufferings personally with an attitude of prayer. Those who negotiate threatening systems daily need the support of listening and accompanying care. A minister's knowledge about and love for her parishioners directly expresses the knowledge and love of God.

Yet, even in pastoral care circumstances that are taxing, there are times for playfulness, humor, and joy.[1] In the midst of exploring personal questions through the lens of faith, there is a deep satisfaction and often a felt sense of the presence of God. Such a form of partnership is often profoundly rewarding.

Pastoral care is a form of lived theology, and in this concluding chapter, we examine scenarios where confession is more appropriate than lament, and describe the purpose of pastoral care: to build a community of support for otherwise lonely people. It is important to care personally about another's story, and yet one can care too much. We have explored scenarios that require referral, and now we offer ways to evaluate whether story care has been effective.

Throughout the book, caregivers have struggled with the question of whether they are adequate to the task of caregiving, seen in the profound and delicate work of pastoral care and counseling. In some scenarios, caregivers have been blessed with just the right kind of training, such as Pastor Janelle's knowledge of domestic violence and Father Roger's familiarity with addiction treatment modalities and centering prayer. In the suicide scenario, Father Bill felt less confident in his abilities to face suicide, but he approached the issue with the proper respect and care, moving toward the pain rather than running from it. Likewise, in Pastor Janelle's care for Kevin, it was not clear initially why he wanted to talk with her, making it hard to assess and respond to his needs. Ultimately, through attention and presence, she was able to discover the meaning that he was making at this difficult point in his life.

THE DELICATE AND VULNERABLE TASK OF MEANING-MAKING

Let us explore the perseverance that is required to care for stories of suffering on the frontlines of widespread cultural pain. The patience described is a fruit of spiritual practice that fosters a trust in God.[2] People of different faiths can provide pastoral care for one another, and God is present where the longing and vulnerability intersect. Hope is born in seemingly hopeless suffering through the care for stories, systems, and selves.

One way is to name what others have silenced. Taboo topics that are not often the subject of polite conversation in religious communities inform the primary material of this book. As a result, pastoral care is a site of joy, precisely because such forbidden topics are being faced rather than avoided. Pastoral care opens the creative and transcendent horizon in people's lives, naming how they have worked to resist trauma and suffering. Gathered around the witness of the life, death, and resurrection of Jesus Christ, its message is faith made real through interaction with suffering.

When interpersonal harm takes place—such as in suicide or addiction—care is required. "Where is God when I am suffering?" "How can I be saved from the harm I have done to others and myself?" These theological questions raised by human harm are among the most complex theological questions. New research indicates that trauma has communal dimensions that are easily seen in Scripture.[3] Understanding the interpersonal harm described in the stories is a delicate task of interpretation of harm and requires the best listening with a spirit attuned for the presence of grace.

The central theme of the book has been that theology is lived out in the soul's laments as the suffering struggle through challenging times. Listening deeply to such laments changes the minister and the careseeker. When ministers come alongside human suffering with the desire to hear stories, they cannot predict the outcome in the faith lives of those they counsel. Rather, they can attend along the way, noting the changes that occur because of being heard through suffering.

CAPACITY FOR WITNESS

The key theological idea that ministers do not bring faith to any life scenario, but that God is already present in the moment, reconfigures the position of the pastoral caregiver to that of an attentive witness. Witnesses watch and confirm what has happened rather than changing the subject, and their actions occur because of the conviction that God is active in the world.

Understanding that each person is created in the image of God, with inalienable dignity and vocation, provides a new basis for the witnessing that occurs in pastoral care and counseling. Because of the implicit presence of God, caregivers become attentive to the seemingly mundane face-to-face conversations that are acts of care. Some might not feel that they are doing much by listening, but by honoring the reality of what someone else experienced, one becomes a witness.[4] Witnessing as an act of listening with sacred attention to the multiple manifestations of harm is the beginning of healing for many who have faced silenced pain.

God's call to live in community involves one's entire social identity: race, class, sexual orientation, and disability; understanding the aspects of social identity through pastoral care can help people live out their faith. Living lives of engagement across different social identities requires attentiveness, patience, and a willingness to make mistakes.

Some people are made vulnerable because of oppression— because their social position means they have less power. Others are vulnerable because their bodies age and are prone to disease. Pastoral care does not presume able-bodiedness but engages with disability and difference, working in the very arena where vulnerability and need arise. People with a range of human and social capacities are all like-wise created in the image of God. Through relationships of trust and care, people can come to know the image of God in one another; thus, the activity of God can be revealed in human experience.

An all-too-natural response to vulnerability is to deny it and escape into perfectionism. Yet, in the attempt to deny vulnerability, one also risks silencing the space in the soul that is meant to communion with others and God. Embracing inevitable vulnerability requires humor and grace. Those who have done so earn trust easily. The capacity for vulnerability precedes and undergirds pastoral care.

RESTORING THE INTERPERSONAL BRIDGE

When people are not allowed to be vulnerable, they lose the ability to sustain meaningful relationships. Building relationships has been described as creating an interpersonal bridge.[5] Such bridges exist among people and with God. When trust is destroyed, the interpersonal bridge is broken; yet the interpersonal bridge can also be repaired over time. People can construct bridges to other individuals, to communities, and to God.

Pastoral care and counseling restores interpersonal bridges between people and God. Young children cared for by caregivers emerge with a stable sense of self because a bridge has been built to them. With the misuse of power, the interpersonal bridges of an entire community can be broken, such as the eroded trust between Father George and his community. Such violations take a long time to repair since they involve repairing the communal narratives' ruptured attachment.

The slow process of pastoral care and counseling rehabilitates trust to create a calm and centered space amid life's daily trials. A sign that the space has occurred is when there is a reliable feeling of "you exist" when talking to another.[6] The conviction leads to the next step in community—*because you exist, then you can choose in a moment to be honest and serve together.* Vulnerability and service require establishing deep trust—what, in the early chapters, was called being kept in mind by one another and remembered by God. This arena is where the fruits of the Spirit begin to be evident in human life (Gal 5:22–23).

At times, a pastoral caregiver listening to a despairing other builds a bridge to them. At other times, God holds careseekers, knitting together their broken parts. Most often, pastoral caregivers collaborate with God to be witnesses to human suffering for healing. In so doing, Christ's purposes take on human form, and the Holy Spirit, as both comforter and advocate, creates the space for human healing and growth. The primary way the Holy Spirit works in pastoral care is through helping people truthfully witness one another's experience.

VOCATION AND PRAYER

The notion of vocation throughout the book emphasizes that God blesses people where they are while also calling them to something better.[7] Vocation refers to much more than a job. Even people who do not labor in full-time employment can exercise their vocation by living with purpose. Understanding that God oversees *final things* gives believers hope that holds them and gives them a direction forward.[8] During Samantha's struggle with addiction, she learned to discover her purpose and trust that God held the future. One of the greatest gifts of ministry is helping people to discover their unique vocation amid oppression and suffering, helping people believe in a future that is more than they could have imagined alone, a future held by God.

Even though some of the book's case studies appeared to be counseling stories only, they are parables about the spiritual life, the everyday disciplines of joy and surrender that are central to the Christian practice of faith. Prayer, that ultimate ground of the Spirit, is thus an essential element of these stories.[9] Estela prayed for Clara and thus cared for her helplessness when Clara did not come back to the food pantry. Father Bill prayed for Ralph and June, thus holding inexpressible pain. When James prayed for his daughter, Samantha, he let go and helped her flourish without fear.

Prayer is not conscious contact between self-aware persons and a manifest God; it is contact between the unconscious selves of people and God's hiddenness. Prayer is more than can be stated; it is a divine mystery existing before creation that gets further away the more it is defined. Prayer does not just fill in the suffering in human life or ask us to make a courageous choice that bypasses the intellect. Instead, prayer gives us the awareness that God's presence fills the universe and that God goes on creating all the time so that humankind can exist. God is as close to the person as the rhythm of their breath.

Faithful people often search for God's purposes in the harm that comes to them, looking for signs of a plan. Often, the worst abuses of pastoral care preempt questioning with easy answers, "Why did bad things happen to me when I am a good person?" When a minister provides answers too quickly to a person who needs to discover the answers themselves, as in the idea that this "happened for a reason," she can preempt hope. Pastoral care does not answer dilemmas of meaning but dwells in them, focusing on deepening the significance rather than giving solutions, thereby restoring the interpersonal bridge. This is done with an attitude of mystery and attentiveness to the person's own answers, directly asking them what has happened to them through their suffering and how they understand it.

At other times, people do not have strong self-worth and do not sense that they deserve anything different from the terrible things that have happened to them. In this case, people often need a set of mirrors through which to see themselves with a sense of dignity. Sometimes ministers might need to help these careseekers feel that they deserve to ask such bold questions of God and that God will answer. Equipping people without a sense of dignity to lament to God requires giving them a holy boldness that is based on the image of God created in them as well as offering them a place to ask the questions.

GENRE MISTAKES IN PASTORAL CARE

At times, ministers believe that a careseeker wants a listening ear, when, in fact, the careseeker wants forgiveness from God. In this genre mistake, a minister can use the important skills taught throughout the book to build attachment to the careseeker when that person wants to be introduced to the practices of the church—in the Protestant tradition, the communal confession of sins and absolution, and in the Catholic tradition, the confessional and the final rites. Such practices give sinful people a chance to live into God's grace.

Certainly the reverse can also be true. People can be given the rites of the church when all they wanted first was a conversation. At times, families are dismayed when a priest does the last rites without seeming to notice them as people or greet them as persons. Some of the best priests combine wise conversation with family members around the last rites in order to meet pastoral care needs as well as theological needs. For wise ministers, the sacrament and pastoral conversation belong to a sacred whole, linking conversation with the practice of faith.

People need to be taught the richness and meaning of their sacramental traditions, learning that they are not a simplistic ticket to heaven but are rather an expression of an ongoing life of faith and witness to the good news.[10] In ordinary life events, people long for the rites and activities of the church to be translated into their everyday experience. For the overscrupulous person, it could mean accepting the forgiveness of sins as a way of not being burdened by shame from the past. Often people are haunted by a pervasive emptiness and frequently need help putting together a life that is meaningful, discovering hopes and dreams, and being reconnected to community. Religious traditions help fill emptiness, but only when they are translated in ways that make sense for the new cultural situation.

Because the human community belongs to God and is rooted in God's presence, people can become responsible to and serve one another. Religious traditions have practices for fostering such knowledge. The Franciscan practice of contemplating the crucifixion brings an awareness of the finitude and joy in the face of sin. The awareness of sin is not individualistic or self-serving but paradoxically leads to advocacy. The liberation practice of Bible study in grassroots Christian communities leads to transformative action and a deep sense of God's active peace that works for justice. Preaching and serving at the table impact how people understand God and thus have concrete and practical ramifications as acts of pastoral care. Understanding how all are created in God's image and interpreting Christ's unjust suffering in the right fashion leads us to take the marginalized person off the cross whenever possible.[11]

CARE SO THAT PEOPLE DO NOT DIE ALONE

While working at a hospital on the border of the United States and Mexico, I saw too many people die alone in the intensive care unit. John Does, as they are called in the hospital, were cut off from community, suffering and dying without witnesses. I was deeply impacted by their ordinary and silenced human tragedy. This led me to continue to study and practice pastoral care, believing that it is essential to rebuild the bridges of attachment and community between people and their friends and family while there is still time. I am convinced that *the time between birth and death is the brief window that is available to allow love to grow in our lives.* If we continue to learn and teach the lessons of pastoral care, fewer people will die alone. The aim of the stories shared in this book is to restore bonds of community so that people who have been estranged from relationship can be joined slowly back into community.

The situation of dying friendless and alone, without a social identity, is often the result of multiple harms that have been done by individuals and others as well as social suffering stemming from oppression. The cumulative suffering in such scenarios can be hard to comprehend. That restoration begins with Jesus Christ, who died alone and in doing so created human community that meant others should not have to suffer. Nevertheless, this book is not about death and dying, but about living, and continuing to engage through the many cumulative practices that alleviate estrangement and despair.

God listens to us, both as individuals and as members of community, amid the estrangement that humans face. Being an individual created in God's image, regardless of what we can do or have been able to perform, means that each person is called beyond their current horizon. Constantly negotiating what it means to live in relationship to God and be remembered by God in their struggles, a person whose life conflicts have been hidden needs help in feeling that God hears that person. Pastoral care and counseling actively remembers forgotten and silenced stories through the mystery of God's presence.

My implicit argument is that human connection and relationship are the most important aspects of existence. When I worked as a hospice chaplain, for example, no one told me that they wished they had worked more in middle adulthood. Pastoral care is a discipline that can help people discern what matters the most and live into this identity. Nearing death, cumulative bonds of life become apparent, so viewing things from the standpoint of death is powerfully clarifying and leads people to focus on what matters most in life. Thus, helping people discern how to live in the most meaningful ways is part of the aim of pastoral care. My convictions arise out of the deep respect for human bonds and connection, how our bonds shape identity, and what can be done when they break down.

Conclusion

ENTAILMENT IN ANOTHER'S STORY
AND THE CAPACITY TO CARE

People who begin pastoral care and counseling often wonder if they will be able to say the right thing in the face of intractable suffering. It is okay to say "I'm sorry for what you're going through" when witnessing a painful experience, provided this is an authentic response and not a way to avoid pain. Witnessing, crying out to God, and helping people lament are more helpful than giving answers or quick advice. The beginning of care is seeing what another person is going through and acknowledging how that pain must hurt. It is not important to have been through the same pain to give an authentic acknowledgment.

Underneath all pastoral care and counseling is an attitude of respect for the human journey, no matter how difficult that journey has been. Early in the book, we explored the capacity for "pastoral imagination," that ability to interpret life through ministry experience in conversation with Scripture and other sources to the end of social transformation.[12] Pastoral imagination understands that all God's children have meaningful lives. In this section, we describe a crucial aspect of this pastoral imagination that has been implicit in the book.

The ability to care about another person's story often includes some element of conversion—being changed by another's story. The capacity to be changed by the story of another is *entailment*, that sense that what matters in another person's story matters to me. This can be costly at times; it can feel like a burden. Entailment is the opposite of self-serving interest, wherein one listens to the stories of others to become an "expert" on something or add an experience to a resumé. It is also different from checking off boxes on an intake form.

If a person has the capacity for entailment, it is clear to mentors and ministry supervisors; if a person does not have the quality, it can be hard to teach. A recent book in the field of pastoral care and counseling, *Listening and Caring Skills*, describes how caring is a skill that can be taught.[13] Some ministers are natural listeners, but can one become more caring? Caring requires entailment; listening can be a means to another end, such as selling a product.

Indeed, *caring* is a dispensation more than a skill. At the heart of caring is a fundamental transformation of the caregiver. The caregiver cannot go about life in the same fashion once the story is heard.

When one is changed by becoming entailed, the caregiver must go in a different direction. In a multiplier effect, when people become entailed in each other's stories, a community is formed around stories. The definition of *community* is "the ability to share each other's stories as one's own." Because of the way story care functions, the formation of religious community happens when people become entailed with each other's stories and start to care for others' narratives in new ways.

Vicarious trauma is the condition in which one experiences diminished spirituality because of powerlessness to solve another's problem. Compassion fatigue is when one feels overwhelmed by another's story and loses faith, but entailment is different. Entailment involves inspiration or the empowerment that comes from witnessing, a new vitality that issues from understanding someone else's experience rather than shutting down through fear or defensiveness.[14]

Chronic exposure to the kinds of stories we have explored, such as narratives of addiction, undocumented immigration, spousal abuse, and suicide, may overwhelm caregivers if they do not build networks with other supportive caregivers who understand the distinctive burdens that come from engaging this kind of suffering. Consequently, entailment shared with others becomes community. Entailment empowers the other based on the transformation that has taken place in oneself. Then caregivers need to enter networks with others who understand the specific losses and challenges of their distinctive ministry contexts (e.g., ministry with veterans) to share their challenges with others who understand. Ministers who become entailed by the stories of others build coalitions for change, using empathy to connect with others who care about similar concerns.

Compassionate and engaged story care honors the distinctiveness of someone's knowledge of life, their loves and friendships, the joys and delights that are as unique as fingerprints. By noting that one is entailed in another's story does not mean taking over that uniqueness or subsuming another's story to one's own. Rather, entailment is the way pastoral care changes caregivers. When a person experiences entailment in another person's story, they are keeping faith with that memory of suffering, holding it before God even as they listen to the contours of its narrative.

EARNING TRUST, SHARING YOUR OWN STORY, AND REFERRING

Pastoral care relationships sometimes require careseekers to name their own need for care. Such vulnerability is possible if someone has experienced care in the past and has been able to establish a trusting relationship. Until trust is earned, pastoral care cannot exist. There will be times when ministers witness the most severe forms of suffering: accidents, trauma, and violence, yet until they have earned trust, it will be difficult to be invited into a deeper experience of story care. Some ministers write annual condolence cards after a loss but may not be invited to hear a story about that loss until two or three years later.

The faithfulness of ministry means being present to the untold story until someone asks a question of meaning or until a caregiver reaches out with a request for pastoral care. Ministers need to be attuned to hearing such requests under the surface of everyday language since people often do not come out directly and say, "I need to talk with you about this problem." Yet the ability to ask for and receive help often starts the process of pastoral care. Without a counselee, there can be no pastoral counseling.

At times, ministers step into painful territory in their own story care by caring for parishioners. They might counsel an abuse victim when they themselves are child abuse survivors. They might counsel other children of alcoholics when they are also the children or parents of alcoholics themselves. How does a minister know when it is possible to *use* this experience, not sharing their own story but allowing it to inform care, so that they can be a better caregiver? Also, if this is not possible, the minister simply needs to refer the care to another.

Someone who is immediately flooded with emotion and starts crying uncontrollably when they encounter a loss may not be effective at providing pastoral care for a person's story. It is at this time that a minister may need to refer, giving the person the proper counselor's contact or even attending the first appointment with them. Shared experience can be helpful, provided the minister does not start to share their own seemingly similar narrative. Indeed, only if a minister can keep from being completely overwhelmed by the feelings from their own story can they be effective in the care for another. Slipping into advice giving, which can shade into bossiness, is another sign that a caregiver is feeling overwhelmed and may not be able to hear and feel the stories that matter to another.

SIGNS OF EFFECTIVE STORY CARE

We can be certain that the signs of story care have been effective when a story begins to feel like it *belongs* to the careseeker. All too often people move through life as if a series of random events are happening to them. The type of pastoral care outlined in this book helps a person to understand the turning points in their life, clarifying the shape of one's life and importance of key events. Realizing the complex influences of families, social factors, personal skills, and abilities means that a person will grasp a deeper sense of the meaning of their own life in faith and be able to claim their stories as their own.

At times, people's lives feel determined by one overarching story about a moment of trauma or harm that has occurred at the hand of another. Furthermore, when people feel abused or harmed by another, their story can be covered by a layer of self-doubt and self-denigration. Pastoral care is a determined, supportive ministry that listens to the contours of people's lives so that they can experience the love and care of God. When a caregiver listens to a story, they are looking for the presence of a self, someone who can understand their own strengths and failings, a child of God who, at the same time, is far from perfect. Sometimes, in religious communities, people want to complain about each other or enlist a minister to fix another. Their perspectives are only "one side of the story," and it is important to surround the narratives with enough distance so that someone can sense that you understand them without "taking their side."

Stories belong to the great arc of human memory. Telling them can be like resting on a riverbank long enough to allow the river to pass by. In listening to stories, ministers are positional as witnesses to the pain and sorrow of a careseeker. By knowing and holding what is private, ministers help human pain be held in the memory of God. As John Bell's powerful hymn states, "Your hands, though bloodied on the cross, survive to hold and heal and warn."[15] Because pastoral care takes place under the sign of the cross—at its feet in every encounter—it can hold together the complexity and immensity of harm before God, thereby restoring community.

MYSTERY IN PASTORAL CARE

Ministry is more than a single technique. It is a process through which suffering is transformed by being witnessed to in the presence of the cross. It is a practice of care in which people surround one another with ministries of mercy even as they are surrounded by God. Although pastoral counselors often emphasize the healing effects of their specific modalities of treatment, new evidence indicates that *it is relationship that heals*. Ministry relationships heal by remembering the deepest longings of the human spirit. Keeping faith with memories of suffering through conversation helps hold together disparate parts of human experience.

Ordinary church life, with its preaching and sacraments, meets the person at each stage of the cycle of life, from birth to death, with the notion that God witnesses to them and sees their suffering. On the one hand, the ordinary pastoral care of a congregation or parish has an important role in meeting attachment needs even as it meets spiritual needs. Pastoral counseling, on the other hand, is that disciplined attention to the story that helps a person make sense out of it and believe that their story belongs to them.

Pastoral care and counseling is an orientation to human experience that is interested in stories and dwells in mystery, not needing to come to quick conclusions about life. The attitude of the caregivers explored throughout is one of accompaniment, soft challenge, and sharing burdens. By orienting all ministry in this fashion, hospitals and churches can enrich the source of inspiration and deepen the experience of pastoral ministry.

The conviction that the human person is made for communion with others and with God is a central conviction that emerges from each story. Rather than being an isolated individual who struggles to compete and define themselves, people are primarily in relationship to one another.

Churches and ministries of mercy such as nonprofits and hospitals should first require ministers to be self-aware. By grasping some of the unconscious motivations for ministry—the ways that one needs to be needed—a minister will provide wiser and more effective care that is less likely to lead to burnout.

Ministers always balance the pastoral care needs of individuals with services of worship and acts of justice. Pastoral care is inextricable from worship and service, but that it is also a distinctive moment in Christian practice deserves full attention and articulation. Believing that it is a moment of lived theology, I maintain that pastoral care is more like lament than exhortation, and that ministers help create the conditions in which God's presence becomes known through hearing the contours of the human story.

The central element in the practice of pastoral care is *patience*, a virtue that is undervalued in a culture that expects problems to be fixed quickly. Since the problems that people face are often deeply interwoven within destructive patterns, family dynamics, and social systems, people feel despair if pastoral care is approached as an immediate conversion rather than accompaniment on a long journey toward resolution.

Pastoral care is a journey in which people come closer to God while coming closer to one another. The ancient theologian Dorotheus of Gaza imagined the life of faith as rotating in a concentric circle, drawing nearer to God. In this process, as people draw near to God, they also draw nearer to one another. Those who wish to understand God's story of love and care for the world must become closer to one another's despair even as they draw closer to God. Becoming entailed in their stories—and changed by them in profound ways—will thus bring a person closer to the wonder and mystery of God.

The most important tone of pastoral care is mystery, the delicate balance of not knowing and wanting to understand someone else's experience. A not-knowing attitude keeps us in touch with the mystery of God that is unconscious in our experience. At the same time, through the practice of not knowing, we bear one another's burdens in mystery, even while not fully understanding what we are carrying.

Ultimately, it is because God creates the world and redeems it for God's purposes that pastoral care can continue. The attitude of holding a story, of witnessing to it, and keeping faith with it, means that we can continue to hear such human stories without changing the subject. Through hearing such stories over time, we may become the kind of people worthy of hearing them.

Conclusion

FOR FURTHER REFLECTION

1. Why is pastoral care and counseling more than learning a skill or technique?
2. How is witnessing different from listening?
3. What are some signs that a minister might not be effective in hearing another's story?
4. What are some signs that story care has been effective?

NOTES

INTRODUCTION

1. Kathleen A. Cahalan, *Introducing the Practice of Ministry* (Collegeville, MN: Liturgical Press, 2010), 53.

2. Barbara J. McClure, *Moving beyond Individualism in Pastoral Care and Counseling: Reflections on Theory, Theology, and Practice* (Eugene, OR: Cascade Books, 2010).

3. David Smail, *Power, Interest, and Psychotherapy* (Ross-on-Whye, UK: PCCS Books, 2015).

4. Nancy Pineda Madrid, *Suffering and Salvation in Ciudad Juárez* (Minneapolis: Fortress Press, 2011).

1. PASTORAL CARE CONVERSATIONS

1. As a seminary-trained minister in a parish, Janelle is responsible for day-to-day ministry in that context. In some settings, she would not be eligible for ordination as a clergyperson, but many of her ministerial duties are similar to a parish priest.

2. Craig Dykstra, "Imagination and the Pastoral Life," *Christian Century*, March 8, 2008, 26–31.

3. Dietrich Bonhoeffer, *Life Together: The Classic Exploration of Christian Community* (San Francisco: HarperOne, 2009), 97, quote updated to reflect inclusive language.

4. Bessel Van der Kolk, *The Body Keeps the Score: Brain, Mind, and Body in the Healing of Trauma* (New York: Penguin, 2014), 350.

5. Al Miles, *Domestic Violence: What Every Pastor Needs to Know*, 2nd ed. (Minneapolis: Fortress Press, 2011).

6. Daniel Siegel, *The Developing Mind: How Relationships and the Brain Intersect to Shape Who We Are*, 2nd ed. (New York: Guilford Press, 2015).

7. Leila Scannell and Robert Gifford, "Defining Place Attachment: A Tripartite Organizing Framework," *Journal of Environmental Psychology* 30 (2010): 1–10.

8. Pehr Granqvist and Lee Kirkpatrick, "Attachment and Religious Representations and Behavior," in *Handbook of Attachment: Theory, Research, and Clinical Applications*, ed. Jude Cassidy and Phillip R. Shaver, 3rd ed. (New York: Guilford Press, 2016), 803–22.

9. Wayne Oates, *The Presence of God in Pastoral Counseling* (Nashville: Word Publishers, 1986).

10. Kirk Byron Jones, *Addicted to Hurry: Spiritual Strategies for Slowing Down* (Valley Forge, PA: Judson Press, 2003).

11. Judith Bula Wise, *Empowerment Practice with Families in Distress* (New York: Columbia University Press, 2005), 34.

12. Philip Browning Helsel, *Pastoral Power beyond Psychology's Marginalization: Resisting the Discourses of the Psy-Complex* (New York: Palgrave, 2015).

13. Robert Neimeyer, *Meaning Reconstruction and the Experience of Loss* (Washington, DC: APA Press, 2001).

14. Michael White, *Maps of Narrative Practice* (New York: W. W. Norton, 2007).

15. M. Kathryn Armistead, *God-Images in the Healing Process* (Minneapolis: Fortress Press, 1995), 3.

16. Deborah van Deusen Hunsinger, *Pray without Ceasing: Revitalizing Pastoral Care* (Grand Rapids, MI: Eerdmans, 2006).

2. FEELING REMEMBERED BY GOD

1. Laurence Holben, *All the Way to Heaven: A Theological Reflection on Dorothy Day, Peter Maurin, and the Catholic Worker* (Eugene, OR: Wipf and Stock, 1997), 6.

2. Charles V. Gerkin, *An Introduction to Pastoral Care* (Nashville: Abingdon Press, 1997), 24.

3. Karen Scheib, *Challenging Invisibility: Practices of Care with Older Women* (St. Louis: Chalice Press, 2004).

4. Richard M. Gula, *Just Ministry: Professional Ethics for Pastoral Ministers* (Mahwah, NJ: Paulist Press, 2010), 131.

5. Jeanne Hoeft, L. Shannon Jung, and Joretta Marshall, *Practicing Care in Rural Congregations and Communities* (Minneapolis: Fortress Press, 2010), 58.

6. Steven Levenkron, *Cutting: Understanding and Overcoming Self-Mutilation* (New York: W. W. Norton, 2006), 107.

7. John Patton, *Pastoral Care in Context: An Introduction to Pastoral Care* (Minneapolis: Fortress Press, 2005).

8. Jay Paul Hinds, "The Prophet's Wish: A Freudian Interpretation of Martin Luther King's Dream," *Pastoral Psychology* 61, no. 4 (2012): 470.

9. Mihee Kim-Kort and LeQuita Hopgood Porter, "You're How Old? The Struggle with Ageism," in *Streams Run Uphill: Conversations with Young Clergywomen of Color*, ed. Mihee Kim-Kort (Valley Forge, PA: Judson Press, 2014), 35.

10. Alice Miller, *The Drama of the Gifted Child: The Search for the True Self* (New York: Basic Books, 2007).

11. Eleonore Stump, *Wandering in Darkness: Narrative and the Problem of Suffering* (Oxford: Oxford University Press, 2010), 405.

12. James Ashbrook, *Minding the Soul: Pastoral Counseling as Remembering* (Minneapolis: Fortress Press, 1996), xiii.

13. Jon Allen, *Coping with Trauma: Hope through Understanding* (Washington, DC: APA Press, 2005), 51–52.

14. Bessel van der Kolk, *The Body Keeps Score: Brain, Mind, and Body in the Healing of Trauma* (New York: Penguin Books, 2014), 79.

15. Van der Kolk, *The Body Keeps Score*, 350.

16. Patton, *Pastoral Care in Context*, 30.

17. Dementia is an important subject that is discussed further in chapter 7.

18. John Swinton, *Dementia: Living in the Memories of God* (Grand Rapids, MI: Eerdmans, 2012), 110.

19. Johann Baptist Metz, *A Passion for God: The Mystical-Political Dimension of Christianity*, trans. J. Matthew Ashley (New York: Paulist Press, 1998).

20. Brother Lawrence, *The Practice of the Presence of God* (New Kensington, PA: Whitaker House, 1982).

21. Jean-Pierre de Caussade, *The Sacrament of the Present Moment* (San Francisco: HarperSanFrancisco, 2009).

3. STORIES OF SUICIDE SURVIVORS

1. Robert C. Dykstra, *Discovering a Sermon: Personal Pastoral Preaching* (St. Louis: Chalice Press), 99.

2. Richard Rohlheiser in Hospice Foundation of America's *Journey: A Newsletter to Help in Bereavement* (Summer 2005).

3. Peter Tyler, "The Catholic Mystical Tradition as a Guide to Contemporary Pastoral Care," in *Keeping Faith in Practice: Aspects of Catholic Practical Theology*, ed. James Sweeney, Gemma Simmonds, and David Lonsdale (London: SCM Press, 2010), 149.

4. Monica McGoldrick, *The Genogram Journey: Reconnecting with Your Family* (New York: W. W. Norton, 2011), 75.

5. Simon Shimshon Rubin, Ruth Malkinson, and Eliezer Witztum, *A Clinician's Guide to Working with the Bereaved: Multiple Lenses on Loss and Mourning* (London: Routledge, 2012), 56.

6. Marcello Ferrada-Noli, Marie Asberg, Kari Ormstad, Tom Lundin, and Elisabet Sundo, "Suicidal Behavior after Severe Trauma," *Journal of Traumatic Stress* 11, no. 1 (1998): 103.

7. Melissa M. Kelley, *Grief: Contemporary Theory and the Practice of Ministry* (Minneapolis: Fortress Press, 2010), 12.

8. Michael White, *Narratives of Therapist's Lives* (Adelaide, South Australia: Dulwich Centre Press, 1997), 61.

9. Rubin, Malkinson, and Witztum, *A Clinician's Guide to Working with the Bereaved*, 23.

10. Kelley, *Grief*, 25.

11. White, *Narratives of Therapist's Lives*, 56.

12. Jon Allen, *Coping with Trauma*, 2nd ed. (Washington, DC: American Psychiatric Publishing, 2004), 76.

13. Paula Boss, *Ambiguous Loss: Learning to Live with Unresolved Grief* (Cambridge: Harvard University Press, 1999), 6.

14. McGoldrick, *The Genogram Journey*, 145.

15. Luke Powery, *Dem Dry Bones: Preaching, Hope, and Death* (Minneapolis: Fortress Press, 2010).

16. Nicholas Wolterstorff, *Lament for a Son* (Grand Rapids, MI: Eerdmans Publishing, 1987).

17. Johann Baptist Metz, *A Passion for God: The Mystical-Political Dimension of Christianity*, trans. J. Matthew Ashley (Mahwah, NJ: Paulist Press, 1999), 42.

18. Blaise Pascal, *Pensées*, Section VII (425).

19. Herdley O. Paolini, "The Development and Use of God Representations in Women" (PhD diss., Western Michigan University, 2001).

20. Ara Norenzayan, Will M. Gervais, and Kali H. Trezsniewski, "Mentalizing Deficits Constrain Belief in God," *PLoS ONE* 7, no. 5 (2012): e36880, doi.org/10.1371/journal.pone.0036880.

21. Henri Nouwen, *The Wounded Healer: Ministry in Contemporary Society* (New York: Random House, 2013), 92.

4. STORIES OF MARGINALIZED PEOPLE

1. Gustavo Gutierrez, *The Power of the Poor in History*, trans. Robert R. Barr (Eugene, OR: Wipf & Stock Publishers, 1983/2004), 18.

2. Charles V. Gerkin, *An Introduction to Pastoral Care* (Nashville: Abingdon Press, 1997), 24.

Notes

3. Emmanuel Y. Lartey, *Pastoral Theology in an Intercultural World* (Cleveland: Pilgrim Press, 2006), 124.

4. Emmanuel Y. Lartey, *In Living Color: An Intercultural Approach to Pastoral Care and Counseling*, 2nd ed. (London: Jessica Kingsley, 2003), 132.

5. Gonzalo Bacigalupe and Kimberly Parker, "Transnational Connections through Emerging Technologies," in *Transitions: The Development of Children of Immigrants*, ed. Carola Suarez-Orozco, Mona Abo-Zena, and Amy Marks (New York: New York University Press, 2015), 61.

6. John Tirman, *Dream Chasers: Immigration and the American Backlash* (Cambridge, MA: MIT Press, 2015).

7. Linda Martín-Alcoff, *Visible Identities: Race, Gender, and the Self* (Oxford: Oxford University Press, 2005).

8. Marcia Alesan Dawkins, *Clearly Invisible: Racial Passing and the Color of Cultural Identity* (Waco, TX: Baylor University Press, 2012).

9. Jeanette Rodriguez, *Stories of Our Lives: Hispanic Women's Spirituality* (Mahwah, NJ: Paulist Press, 1996).

10. Judith Bula Wise, *Empowerment Practice with Families in Distress* (New York: Columbia, 2005), 35.

11. Wise, *Empowerment Practice*, 35.

12. Noel Ignatiev, *How the Irish Became White* (London: Routledge, 1995).

13. David Rappaport, "Empowerment Meets Narrative: Listening to Stories and Creating Settings," *American Journal of Community Psychology* 23, no. 5 (1995): 803.

14. Bryan N. Massangale, *Racial Justice and the Catholic Church* (Maryknoll, NY: Orbis Books, 2010).

15. Carrie Doehring, *The Practice of Pastoral Care: A Postmodern Approach*, 2nd ed. (Louisville: Westminster/John Knox Press, 2015), 41.

16. Philip Browning Helsel, *Pastoral Power beyond Psychology's Marginalization: Resisting the Discourses of the Psy-Complex* (New York: Palgrave Macmillan, 2015), 125.

17. Ada-Maria Isasi-Diaz, "Solidarity and Love of Neighbor in the 1980s," in *Lift Every Voice: Constructing Christian Theologies from the Underside*, ed. Mary Potter Engel and Susan Thistlethwaite (Maryknoll, NY: Orbis Press, 1998), 32.

18. In other words, compassionate action is not a sign of compassion distress or fatigue — burnout that comes from hearing stories of pain — but rather, it is part of the antidote for burnout because it helps you feel as if you can change some of the conditions that contributed to the unjust suffering in the first place.

5. STORIES OF ABUSE SURVIVORS

1. Kevin and Pastor Janelle's narrative was explored across several pastoral counseling sessions. The pastor was able to understand Kevin's story in part because she had previously cared for his mother Pam during a time of marital conflict. This chapter returns to tell the narrative of what occurred in the backstory of Kevin's mother's life, focusing on how she attempted to leave an abusive relationship. If the reader has faced domestic violence, this might be a chapter to take slowly, digesting it with the help of a supportive friend.

2. According to a recent study in an urban area, pastors are frequently sought for counseling after intimate partner violence but are frequently unhelpful in this. Michael Moran, Kevin Flannelly, Andrew Weaver, Jon Overvold, Winifred Hess, and Jo Wilson, "A Study of Pastoral Care, Referral, and Consultation Practices in the New York City Area," *Pastoral Psychology* 53, no. 3 (2005): 255–66.

3. Karolyn Elizabeth Sentner and Karen Caldwell, "Spirituality and the Maintenance of Change: A Phenomenological Study of Women Who Leave Abusive Relationships," *Contemporary Family Therapy* 24, no. 4, (2002): 548.

4. USCCB, "When I Call for Help: A Pastoral Response to Violence against Women," accessed July 12, 2018, http://www.usccb.org/issues-and -action/marriage-and-family/marriage/domestic-violence/when-i-call-for-help .cfm.

5. USCCB, "When I Call for Help."

6. Jeanne M. Hoeft, *Agency, Culture, and Human Personhood* (Eugene, OR: Pickwick Publications, 2009).

7. Hoeft, *Agency, Culture, and Human Personhood.*

8. Carol P. Christ, "Why Don't Feminists Express Anger at God?" *Feminism and Religion blog,* July 9, 2012, https://feminismandreligion.com/2012/ 07/09/why-dont-feminists-express-anger-at-god-by-carol-p-christ/.

9. Dana Crowley Jack, *Silencing the Self: Women and Depression* (Cambridge, MA: Harvard University Press, 1991).

10. Elizabeth Johnson, *She Who Is: The Mystery of God in Feminist Theological Discourse* (New York: Crossroad Publishing, 2002).

11. Mary Allen, *Narrative Therapy for Women Experiencing Domestic Violence* (London: Jessica Kingsley Publishers, 2011).

12. Duane R. Bidwell and Donald L. Batisky, "Identity and Wisdom as Elements of a Spirituality of Hope among Children with End-Stage Renal Disease," *Journal of Childhood and Religion* 2, no. 5 (2011): 20.

13. Sentner and Caldwell, "Spirituality and the Maintenance of Change," 543.

14. Michael White, *Re-Authoring Lives: Interviews and Essays* (Adelaide, Australia: Dulwich Centre Publications, 1995), 99.

Notes

15. Tameka L. Gillum, Cris M. Sullivan, and Deborah I. Bybee, "The Importance of Spirituality in the Lives of Domestic Violence Survivors," *Violence against Women* 12, no. 3 (2006): 240.

16. See https://www.seattle.gov/humanservices/about-us/initiatives/addres sing-domestic-violence-and-sexual-assault (accessed July 13, 2018).

17. Al Miles, *Domestic Violence: What Every Pastor Needs to Know*, 2nd ed. (Minneapolis: Fortress Press, 2011), 25.

18. See http://ncadv.org/learn-more/statistics (accessed July 13, 2018).

19. Pamela Cooper-White, *The Cry of Tamar*, 120.

20. There are other forms of family violence such as child or elder abuse that are beyond the scope of this chapter.

21. Jack, *Silencing the Self*.

22. Shamita Das Dasgupta, "Women's Realities: Defining Violence against Women by Immigration, Race, and Class," in *Violence against Women at the Margins*, ed. Natalie J. Sokoloff and Christina Pratt (New Brunswick, NJ: Rutgers University Press, 2005), 56.

23. See http://avp.org/wp-content/uploads/2017/11/NCAVP-IPV-Report-2016 .pdf (accessed July 13, 2018).

24. Miles, *Domestic Violence*, 16.

25. Jill Davies and Eleanor Lyon, *Domestic Violence Advocacy: Complex Lives/Difficult Choices*, 2nd ed. (Thousand Oaks, CA: Sage Publications, 2013), xx.

26. Jill Davies, Eleanor Lyon, and Diane Monti-Catania, *Safety Planning with Battered Women: Complex Lives/Difficult Choices* (Thousand Oaks, CA: Sage Publications, 2005), 3.

27. Christie Cozad Neuger, *Counseling Women* (Minneapolis: Fortress Press, 2001), 179.

28. Sentner and Caldwell, "Spirituality and the Maintenance of Change," 562.

29. Michael White, *Re-Authoring Lives*, 98–99.

30. I disagree with David W. Augsburger, *Helping People Forgive* (Louisville: Westminster/John Knox Press, 1996) on this point, and argue that what he calls "unilateral forgiveness" is indeed possible without the reconciliation of relationship. In fact, the idea that God is drawing people to reconcile with one another is harmful for someone recovering from an abusive relationship, for whom reconciliation is impossible without a rebalancing of power.

31. Miles, *Domestic Violence*, 128.

32. USCCB, "When I Call for Help: A Pastoral Response to Violence against Women," Washington, DC, November 2002, http://www.usccb.org/ issues-and-action/marriage-and-family/marriage/domestic-violence/when-i -call-for-help.cfm.

33. Miles, *Domestic Violence*, 114–15.

34. To keep faith with the memories of domestic violence, it is important to hold the conviction that God is completely opposed to abuse.

6. STORIES OF ADDICTS AND THEIR FAMILIES

1. David Sheff, *Clean: Overcoming Addiction and Ending America's Greatest Tragedy* (New York: Houghton Mifflin, 2013).
2. Adolescents are not typically part of the pastoral care literature unless there is an entire book devoted to this population.
3. Beverly Conyers, *Everything Changes: Help for Families of Newly Recovering Addicts* (Center City, MN: Hazelden Foundation, 2009).
4. Chris Allen, *Crime, Drugs and Social Theory: A Phenomenological Approach* (London: Routledge, 2017).
5. This approach should be used in tandem with other approaches such as a twelve-step program or cognitive-behavioral therapy, since a one-dimensional approach to addiction is weaker than a multidimensional one.
6. See http://www.smartrecovery.org/professionals/ (accessed July 13, 2018).
7. James O. Prochaska, John C. Norcross, and Carlo C. DiClemente, *Changing for Good: A Revolutionary Six-Stage Program for Overcoming Bad Habits and Moving Your Life Positively Forward* (New York: HarperCollins, 1990), 67.
8. Conyers, *Everything Changes*.
9. Sheff, *Clean*, 103.
10. Mariah Snyder, "Journaling," in *Complementary and Alternative Therapies in Nursing*, ed. Ruth Lindquist, Mariah Snyder, and Mary Frances Tracy, 7th ed. (New York: Springer Publishing, 2014), 210.
11. Gayle Rosellini, *Stinking Thinking* (Centre City, MN: Hazelden, 1985).
12. Augustine, *Confessions* (Bk. 1:1).
13. Kent Dunnington, *Addiction and Virtue: Beyond Models of Disease or Choice* (Downers Grove, IL: InterVarsity Press, 2011). This helpful book explains how addiction can be something one seems to begin willingly and yet also has the dynamics of a disease.
14. Sonia Waters, "Identity in the Empathic Community: Alcoholics Anonymous as a Model Community for Storytelling and Change," *Pastoral Psychology* 64, no. 5 (2015): 770.
15. Wendy Farley, *The Wounding and Healing of Desire: Weaving Heaven and Earth* (Louisville: Westminster/John Knox Press, 2005), 51.
16. Farley, *The Wounding and Healing of Desire*, 51.
17. Irenaeus, *Against Heresies and Fragments from the Lost Writings of Irenaeus* (Boston: Wyatt North Publishing, 2014), 4:20, 7.

18. For a detailed explanation of the Twelve-Step Program of Alcoholics Anonymous, see https://www.aa.org/pages/en_US/twelve-steps-and-twelve-traditions (accessed July 16, 2018).

19. Philip J. Flores, *Addiction as an Attachment Disorder* (New York: Jason Aronson Press, 2011).

20. Sonia Waters, "Identity in the Empathic Community," 770.

21. The idea of defects of character or flaws is not an individualistic moralism that blames the person for the disease of addiction, but rather describes how the personality becomes shaped around addiction practices.

22. Sheff, *Clean*, 105.

23. Only about a third of people who begin a twelve-step program are sober a year later. While those who advocate for the program alone may argue this means they did not work their program, it is also possible that some people require a multidimensional approach to healing from addiction. See Sheff, *Clean*.

24. Conyers, *Everything Changes*, 125.

25. Robert Dykstra, *Counseling Troubled Youth* (Louisville: Westminster/John Knox Press, 1997).

26. Waters, "Identity in the Empathic Community," 790.

27. See http://www.nytimes.com/2013/09/17/science/the-rational-choices-of-crack-addicts.html (accessed July 16, 2018).

28. C. L. Hart, M. Haney, R. W. Foltin, and M. W. Fischman, "Alternative Reinforcers Differentially Modify Cocaine Self-Administration by Humans," *Behavioral Pharmacology* 11, no. 1 (2000): 87.

29. Darren Hill, William J. Penson, and Divine Charura, *Working with Dual Diagnosis: A Psychosocial Perspective* (New York: Palgrave Macmillan, 2016).

30. William R. Miller, Alyssa A. Forceheimes, and Allen Zweben, *Treating Addiction: A Guide for Professionals* (New York: Guilford Press, 2011), 14–16.

31. Sheff, *Clean*.

7. THE SANDWICH GENERATION

1. Lynn Feinberg, Susan C. Reinhard, Ari Houser, and Rita Choula, *Valuing the Invaluable: 2011 Update. The Growing Contributions and Costs of Family Caregiving* (Washington, DC: AARP Public Policy Institute, 2011), https://assets.aarp.org/rgcenter/ppi/ltc/i51-caregiving.pdf.

2. Nancy L. Mace and Peter V. Rabins, *The 36-Hour Day: A Guide to Caring for People Who Have Alzheimer's Disease, Related Dementias, and Memory Loss* (New York: Hachette, 1981/2011), 347.

3. Mace and Rabins, *The 36-Hour Day*, 375.

4. John Swinton, *Dementia: Living in the Memories of God* (Grand Rapids, MI: Eerdmans, 2012), 81.

5. Thomas Keating, *Open Mind, Open Heart* (New York: Continuum, 1986/2006).

6. Anthony Bloom, *Beginning to Pray* (Mahwah, NJ: Paulist Press, 1970), 14.

7. M. Shawn Copeland, *Enfleshing Freedom: Body, Race, and Being* (Minneapolis: Fortress Press, 2009).

8. Bonnie J. Miller-McLemore, *Parenting as Spiritual Practice* (San Francisco: Wiley, 2006), 51.

9. Aelred of Rievaulx, *Spiritual Friendship*, trans. Lawrence C. Braceland, ed. Marsha L. Dutton (Trappist, KY: Cistercian Publications, 2010), 25.

10. Kenda Creasy Dean and Ron Foster, *The Godbearing Life: The Art of Soul Tending for Youth Ministry* (Nashville: Upper Room Books, 1998), 83–84.

11. Tony Jones, *Soul Shaper: Exploring Spirituality and Contemplative Practices in Youth Ministry* (El Cajon, CA: Zondervan/Youth Specialties), 125.

12. Jones, *Soul Shaper*, 122.

13. Kirk Byron Jones, *Addicted to Hurry: Spiritual Strategies for Slowing Down* (Valley Forge, PA: Judson Press, 2003), 26.

14. Margaret Kornfeld, *Cultivating Wholeness: A Guide to Care and Counseling in Faith Communities* (New York: Continuum Publishing, 2012), 282.

15. Donald R. Hands and Wayne L. Fehr, *Spiritual Wholeness for Clergy: A New Psychology of Intimacy with God, Self, and Others* (Lanham, MD: Rowman & Littlefield, 1993).

16. Kornfeld, *Cultivating Wholeness*, 294.

17. Kornfeld, *Cultivating Wholeness*, 283.

18. Jones, *Addicted to Hurry*, 70.

19. Jones, *Addicted to Hurry*, 80.

20. Mother Theresa, *In the Heart of the World: Thoughts, Stories, and Prayers* (Novato, CA: New World Publications, 1997), 20.

21. Kornfeld, *Cultivating Wholeness*, 281.

22. Serene Jones, *Feminist Theory and Christian Theology* (Minneapolis: Augsburg Fortress, 2000), 110.

23. John Calvin, *Institutes of the Christian Religion* (Louisville: Westminster Press, 1960/2006), 1:1.

24. Bonnie J. Miller-McLemore, *In the Midst of Chaos: Caring for Children as Spiritual Practice* (San Francisco: Wiley, 2007).

25. Ewan Kelly, *Personhood and Presence: Self as a Resource for Spiritual and Pastoral Care* (New York: T & T Clark, 2012).

26. Abraham Joshua Heschel, *The Sabbath: Its Meaning for Modern Man* (New York: Farrar, Strauss & Giroux, 1951), 22.

8. STORIES OF CREATING BOUNDARIES

1. James T. O'Reilly and Margaret S. P. Chalmers, *The Clergy Sexual Abuse Crisis and the Legal Responses* (Oxford: Oxford University Press, 2014).

2. Jan Erickson-Pearson, *Healing in Congregations after Clergy Sexual Abuse: A Resource to Assist Synodical Leaders and Local Congregations of the Evangelical Lutheran Church in America* (Chicago: ELCA Division for Ministry, 1997). See also http://download.elca.org/ELCA%20Resource%20Repository/Healing_In_Congregations_After_Clergy_Sexual_Abuse.pdf.

3. Erickson-Pearson, *Healing in Congregations after Clergy Sexual Abuse.*

4. See http://www.kidscenter.org/safe-touch/ (accessed July 17, 2018).

5. Deborah Pope-Lance, "Trauma Intervention: Planning Strategies for Recovery," in *When a Congregation is Betrayed: Responding to Clergy Misconduct*, ed. Candace R. Benyel, Larraine Frampton, Nancy Myer Hopkins, Patricia L. Liberty, and Deborah Pope-Lance (Lexington, KY: Rowman and Littlefield, 2006), 63.

6. Karen Lebacqz and Ronald G. Barton, *Sex in the Parish* (Louisville, KY: Westminster/John Knox Press, 1991), 53.

7. Shirley Glass, *Not "Just Friends": Rebuilding Trust and Recovering Your Sanity after Infidelity* (New York: Free Press, 2003), 10.

8. This statement does not change the fact that ministers are responsible to manage professional boundaries so that they can stay in healthy relationship with their congregations.

9. Of course, there are times when the minister goes through a difficult period and requires the congregation's care, but even in these times, a minister should seek to get their personal needs met outside the congregation.

10. Marie M. Fortune, *Is Nothing Sacred? The Story of a Pastor, the Women He Abused, and the Congregation He Nearly Destroyed* (Eugene, OR: Wipf and Stock, 2008).

11. Cherie Burbach, *Emotional Affairs: How to Prevent, Stop, and Move on From an Emotional Affair* (New York: Bonjour Publishing, 2015).

12. Donald Capps, *Giving Counsel: A Minister's Guidebook* (St. Louis: Chalice Press, 2001), 192.

13. Lebacqz and Barton, *Sex in the Parish*, 15.

14. Pamela Cooper-White, *Shared Wisdom: The Use of the Self in Pastoral Counseling* (Minneapolis: Fortress Press, 2004), 6.

15. Marianne Benkert and Thomas Doyle, "Clericalism, Religious Duress and its Psychological Impact on Victims of Clergy Sexual Abuse," *Pastoral Psychology* 58, no. 3 (2009): 223–38.

16. United States Conference of Catholic Bishops, "Co-Workers in the Vineyard: A Resource for Guiding the Development of Ecclesial Ministry" (Washington, DC, 2005); in many Protestant denominations such as the Presbyterian Church (USA), there is only one kind of minister with distinct functions (lay and ordained).

17. Donald Capps, *The Depleted Self: Sin in a Narcissistic Age* (Minneapolis: Augsburg Fortress Press, 1993).

18. Ronald W. Richardson, *Becoming a Healthier Pastor: Family Systems Theory and the Pastor's Own Family* (Minneapolis: Fortress Press, 2005), 68.

19. Joan E. Hemenway, *Inside the Circle: A Historical and Practical Inquiry Concerning Process Groups in Clinical Pastoral Education* (Decatur, GA: Journal of Pastoral Care Publications, 1996), 183.

20. Philip Culbertson, *Caring for God's People* (Minneapolis: Augsburg Fortress, 2000), 277.

21. Richard M. Gula, *Just Ministry: Professional Ethics for Pastoral Ministers* (Mahwah, NJ: Paulist Press, 2010), 227.

22. Several websites have descriptions of mandated reporting laws in different states, but confidentiality often does not apply to lay ministers outside the space of the confessional.

23. Ronald W. Richardson, *Creating a Healthier Church: Family Systems Theory, Leadership, and Congregational Life* (Minneapolis: Fortress Press, 1996), 91.

24. Fortune, *Is Nothing Sacred?*

25. See http://pres-outlook.org/2013/11/albright-apologizes-offers-lessons-learned-in-sexual-abuse-case/ (accessed July 18, 2018).

CONCLUSION

1. Stephen Pattison, *A Critique of Pastoral Care* (London: SCM, 2000).

2. Of course, it is possible that a caregiver could be inspired by God to do this work while the client or patient is nonreligious and is not converted by the counseling. This sort of interreligious pastoral counseling fulfills all the aims of this book.

3. Elizabeth Boase and Christopher G. Frechette, eds., *Bible through the Lens of Trauma* (Atlanta: SBL Press, 2016).

4. Shelly Rambo, *Spirit and Trauma: A Theology of Remaining* (Louisville: Westminster/John Knox Press, 2010).

5. Gershen Kaufman, *Shame: The Power of Caring* (Rochester, VT: Schenkman Books, 1992).

6. If there is not a preponderance of people in a religious community that have this secure sense of self, the atmosphere of the entire community can be unstable.

Notes

7. Ronald T. Haney, *God within You: Mysticism for the 21st Century* (Bloomington, IN: Authorhouse, 2005), 99.

8. O. Ernesto Valiente, "From Utopia to Eu-topia: Christian Hope in History," in *Hope: Promise, Possibility, and Fulfillment*, ed. Richard Lennan and Nancy Pineda-Madrid (Mahwah, NJ: Paulist Press, 2013), 203.

9. Ann and Barry Ulanov, *Primary Speech: A Psychology of Prayer* (Atlanta: John Knox Press, 1983).

10. Christina Puchalski, *A Time to Listen: Spirituality and the Care for the Dying* (Oxford: Oxford University Press, 2006), 151.

11. Jon Sobrino, *The Principle of Mercy: Taking the Crucified People off the Cross* (Maryknoll, NY: Orbis Books, 1994).

12. Craig Dykstra, "Imagination and the Pastoral Life," *Christian Century* (March 8, 2008): 26–31.

13. John Savage, *Listening and Caring Skills: A Guide for Groups and Leaders* (Nashville: Abingdon Press, 1996).

14. Carrie Doehring, *The Practice of Pastoral Care: A Postmodern Approach*, 2nd ed. (Louisville: Westminster/John Knox Press, 2015), 42. Doehring describes compassion fatigue as being the result of fusion, and advocates for compassion as the solution. In my explanation of entailment, this notion of compassion is further developed to describe the changes that need to take place in the caregiver as the result of hearing stories.

15. Hannah Ward and Jennifer Wild, *Human Rites: Worship Resources for an Age of Change* (NY: Bloomsbury, 1995), 267.

INDEX OF SUBJECTS

Index of Subjects

Sandwich generation, 99, 101, 111, 113

Savoring pace, 103–5, 107–8, 112, 125

Seattle Center for Prevention of Sexual and Domestic Violence, 71

Silence as Sabbath, 101

Silent retreat, xx, 101–2, 105, 113

Social systems, xvi, xx, 52–54, 142

Social therapy, 51, 53–55, 57, 59, 63

Society, xv, xvii, 10, 28, 52, 54–55, 58, 82, 85, 93

Soul abuse, 101

Spiritual director, 13, 25, 39, 102, 105, 125

Spiritual friend, 105–6, 112–13

Spiritual mentorship, 105

Stories, sharing of own, xi, xiv, xxi, 13, 23, 27, 56, 118, 128

Suffering, ix, xi–xiii, xv–xvii, xix, xxii, 8, 20, 22, 27–29, 31, 33–35, 40–41, 43, 52–54, 56, 60–63, 66–67, 78, 100, 108–9, 129–31, 133–39, 141

Suicide survivors, 32, 34–37, 40, 46

Supportive resources, 67

Swinton, John, 28

Sympathy, 59–60, 64, 111

Systemic, xiv, xxi, 52, 71

Systems approach, 81

Termination, 85, 117

Time (*referring to struggling or healing time*), xii, xv, xviii–xxi, 5, 8–10, 12, 15, 34–36, 39, 41, 50, 55–56, 60–63, 70, 82, 91, 101, 103–4, 112, 117–18, 121, 126, 137, 139–42

Transnational families, 53

Trauma
Bereavement, 35–38, 40
Vicarious trauma, 54, 138

Trust, 13–14, 21, 27, 29, 32, 45, 81–83, 87, 89–90, 93–94, 109, 114–18, 120–23, 126–27, 130, 132–33, 139
Reestablishing, 83

Twelve-Step Program, 83, 88–90, 92, 95

Unmet childhood needs, xix, 22, 24–26, 124

Vocation, xvi, xx–xxii, 4, 13–15, 17–19, 22–24, 31, 50, 56, 65, 69–70, 79, 84, 91, 93, 105, 128, 131, 133

Witness, xi, xiii–xiv, xvi, 4–5, 17, 22, 28–29, 32, 34–35, 39–40, 61, 130, 131, 133, 135

Woman-defined advocacy, 73, 78